Understanding,
Developing,
and Writing
Effective IEPs

*This book is dedicated to my wife, Jackie,
and my two children, Jacqueline and Scott,
who provide me with the love and purpose for
undertaking projects that I hope will enhance the lives of
others. My life has been blessed by their loving presence.
I also dedicate this book to my parents, who provided me with
the secure and loving foundation from which to grow; my sister,
Carol, who makes me smile and laugh; and my brother-in-law, George,
who has always been a positive guiding light in my professional journey.*

—R. P.

*This book is dedicated to my wife, Anita,
and two children, Collin and Brittany, who give me the
greatest life imaginable. The long hours and many years
it took to finish this book would never have been possible
without the support of my loving wife. Her constant encouragement,
understanding, and love provide me with the strength I need to
accomplish my goals. I thank her with all my heart. I also dedicate
this book to my parents, who have given me support and guidance
throughout my life. Their words of encouragement and guidance
have made my professional journey a rewarding and successful experience.*

—G. G.

A STEP-BY-STEP GUIDE FOR EDUCATORS

Understanding, Developing, and Writing Effective IEPs

ROGER PIERANGELO ~ GEORGE GIULIANI

CORWIN PRESS
A SAGE Publications Company
Thousand Oaks, CA 91320

For information:

Corwin Press
A SAGE Publications Company
2455 Teller Road
Thousand Oaks, California 91320
www.corwinpress.com

SAGE Publications Ltd.
1 Oliver's Yard
55 City Road
London, EC1Y 1SP
United Kingdom

SAGE Publications India Pvt. Ltd.
B 1/I 1 Mohan Cooperative
    Industrial Area
Mathura Road, New Delhi 110 044
India

SAGE Publications Asia-Pacific Pte. Ltd.
33 Pekin Street #02-01
Far East Square
Singapore 048763

Printed in the United States of America

Library of Congress Cataloging-in-Publication Data

Pierangelo, Roger.
Understanding, developing, and writing effective IEPs : a step-by-step guide for educators / Roger Pierangelo, George Giuliani.
    p. cm.
Includes bibliographical references and index.
ISBN 978-1-4129-5421-1 (cloth)
ISBN 978-1-4129-1786-5 (pbk.)
    1. Individualized education programs—United States—Handbooks, manuals, etc.
2. Children with disabilities—Education—United States—Handbooks, manuals, etc.
I. Giuliani, George A., 1938- II. Title.

LC4031.P489 2007
371.9'046—dc22   2006103445

This book is printed on acid-free paper.

07 08 09 10 11 10 9 8 7 6 5 4 3 2 1

Acquisitions Editor:	Allyson P. Sharp
Editorial Assistant:	Nadia Kashper
Production Editor:	Laureen A. Shea
Copy Editor:	Geoffrey T. Garvey
Typesetter:	C&M Digitals (P) Ltd.
Proofreader:	Penny Sippel
Cover Designer:	Michael Dubowe

Contents

Preface

*U*nderstanding, Developing, and Writing Effective IEPs: A Step-by-Step Guide for Educators is intended to provide technical assistance for educators, parents, and others who develop individualized education programs (IEPs) for students with disabilities. The IEP ensures that a student with a disability receives a free appropriate public education (FAPE) in the least restrictive environment (LRE). This guide will assist the IEP team in developing a meaningful, functional plan to help meet the student's unique needs.

The following basic beliefs guided the development of this book:

- The IEP is
  - The most important legal document written for students with disabilities
  - Developed together through discussion at a team meeting
- More than a collection of papers, the IEP is
  - A process that is just as important as the product
  - A communication tool between parents, school, and others
  - An opportunity for parents of students with special needs, guardians, and school personnel to work together as equals
  - A method for joint planning, problem solving, and decision making

The content of this guide is taken from the Individuals with Disabilities Education Act (IDEA) and numerous state statutes with their implementing regulations. Both state and federal law identify the required elements of the IEP. This guide provides descriptions and models for all the required elements of the IEP from present level of educational performance (PLEP) through placement.

Acknowledgments

In the course of writing this book, we have encountered many professional and outstanding sites. Those resources have contributed and continue to contribute enormous information, support, guidance, and education to parents, students, and professionals in the area of special education. Although we have accessed many worthwhile sites, we especially thank and acknowledge the National Dissemination Center for Children with Disabilities, the New York State Department of Education, the Alaska State Department of Education, and the National Institutes of Health.

Dr. Roger Pierangelo and Dr. George Giuliani extend sincere thanks to Allyson Sharp and Laureen Shea at Corwin Press. Their constant encouragement and professionalism made this project a very worthwhile and rewarding experience. We also thank Geof Garvey for his professional editorial contributions to this book.

Roger Pierangelo: I extend thanks to the following: the faculty, administration, and staff of the Department of Graduate Special Education and Literacy at Long Island University; Ollie Simmons, for her friendship, loyalty, and great personality; the students and parents of the Herricks Public Schools I have worked with and known over the past thirty-five years; the late Bill Smyth, a truly gifted and "extraordinary ordinary" man; and Helen Firestone, for her influence on my career and her tireless support of me.

George Giuliani: I extend sincere thanks to all of my colleagues at Hofstra University in the School of Education and Allied Human Services. I am especially grateful to those who have made my transition to Hofstra University such a smooth one, including Maureen Murphy (dean), Daniel Sciarra (chairperson), Frank Bowe, Diane Schwartz (graduate program director of early childhood special education), Darra Pace, Gloria Wilson, Alan Wenderoff, Laurie Johnson, Joan Bloomgarden, Jamie Mitus, Estelle Gellman, Joseph Lechowicz, Holly Seirup, Adele Piombino, Marjorie Butler, Eve Byrne, and Linda Cappa. I also thank my brother and sister, Roger and Claudia; mother-in-law Ursula Jenkeleit; sisters-in-law Karen and Cindy; and brothers-in-law Robert and Bob. They have provided me with encouragement and reinforcement in all of my personal and professional endeavors.

Corwin Press gratefully acknowledges the contributions of the following reviewers:

Shannon Acker
NBCT, Exceptional Needs Specialist
Shelby County Schools
Alabaster, AL

Rachel Aherns
Collaborative Special Education Teacher—Level 1
Johnston Community School District—Summit Middle School
Johnston, IA

Mary L. Jackson
Resource Teacher
Roosevelt Elementary School
Kingsport, TN

Tracy Teaff
Assistant Professor, Technology and Cognition
University of North Texas
Dallas, TX

About the Authors

Roger Pierangelo, PhD, is an associate professor in the Department of Special Education and Literacy at Long Island University. He has been an administrator of special education programs, served for eighteen years as a permanent member of Committees on Special Education, has over thirty years of experience in the public school system as a general education classroom teacher and school psychologist, and serves as a consultant to numerous private and public schools, PTA, and SEPTA groups. Dr. Pierangelo has also been an evaluator for the New York State Office of Vocational and Rehabilitative Services and a director of a private clinic. He is a New York State–licensed clinical psychologist, a certified school psychologist, and a Board Certified Diplomate Fellow in Student and Adolescent Psychology and Forensic Psychology. Dr. Pierangelo is the executive director of the National Association of Special Education Teachers (NASET) and an executive director of the American Academy of Special Education Professionals (AASEP). He also holds the office of vice president of the National Association of Parents with Children in Special Education (NAPCSE).

Dr. Pierangelo earned his BS from St. John's University, MS from Queens College, Professional Diploma from Queens College, PhD from Yeshiva University, and Diplomate Fellow in Student and Adolescent Psychology and Forensic Psychology from the International College of Professional Psychology. Dr. Pierangelo is a member of the American Psychological Association, New York State Psychological Association, Nassau County Psychological Association, New York State Union of Teachers, and Phi Delta Kappa.

Dr. Pierangelo is the author of multiple books by Corwin Press, including *The Big Book of Special Education Resources* and *The Step-by-Step Series for Special Educators.*

George Giuliani, JD, PsyD, is a full-time tenured associate professor and the director of Special Education at Hofstra University's School of Education and Allied Human Services in the Department of Counseling, Research, Special Education, and Rehabilitation. Dr. Giuliani earned his BA from the College of the Holy Cross, MS from St. John's University, JD from City University Law School, and PsyD from Rutgers University, the Graduate School of Applied and Professional Psychology. He earned Board Certification as a Diplomate Fellow in Student and Adolescent Psychology and Forensic Psychology from the International College of Professional Psychology. Dr. Giuliani is also a New York State–licensed psychologist and certified school psychologist and has an extensive private practice focusing on students with special needs. He is a member of the American Psychological Association, New York State Psychological Association, National Association of School Psychologists, Suffolk County Psychological Association, Psi Chi, American Association of University Professors, and the Council for Exceptional Students.

Dr. Giuliani is the president of the National Association of Parents with Children in Special Education (NAPCSE), executive director of the National Association of Special Education Teachers (NASET), and executive director of the American Academy of Special Education Professionals (AASEP). He is a consultant for school districts and early childhood agencies and has provided numerous workshops for parents and guardians and teachers on a variety of special education and psychological topics. Dr. Giuliani is the coauthor of numerous books by Corwin Press, including *The Big Book of Special Education Resources* and *The Step-by-Step Series for Special Educators.*

Introduction

The Individual with Disabilities Education Act of 2004 (IDEA 2004) requires that all students with disabilities in need of special education services be provided with free appropriate public education designed to meet their unique needs. The cornerstone of this provision is the development and implementation of the **individualized education program (IEP).** The IEP serves as a written agreement between the parents and the school system. According to the regulations, the IEP must be developed at a meeting at which parent and school personnel *jointly* make decisions about the student's program, and it must be reviewed and revised at least annually.

The IEP serves a number of purposes, such as providing a vehicle for communication, problem resolution, and compliance. It also provides goals and objectives based on the general curriculum to guide the special education services to be provided in the **least restrictive environment (LRE)** and outlines the type and amount of such services. Although the IEP itself consists of numerous parts, the goals are considered the foundation of the plan and should serve as a blueprint for the student's instructional program. The IEP is a necessary resource for all teachers who are responsible for implementing the IEP and planning daily, weekly, and monthly instructional activities for the student with a disability. The IEP should not be regarded as just a compliance document. Administrators and IEP team members must remember that it takes time to develop an appropriate IEP that can guide instruction.

1

Foundational Issues in Individualized Education Programs (IEPs)

Introduction

One of the major responsibilities of special education is the development and writing of the individualized education program (IEP) for a student with a disability. The IEP is a required legal document that outlines and defines the school district's goals, supports, and services for any student who has been classified as having a disability and is receiving special education services. Being classified as a student with a disability requires a series of steps, often referred to as the special education process. This process

- Identifies the student as being suspected of having a disability
- Assesses and evaluates the student to determine the severity and types of problems that he or she may be encountering that prevents him or her from succeeding in school
- Determines the specific type of disability that the student may have (that is, specific learning disabilities, autism)

- Identifies the least restrictive environment for the student's disability
- Defines the types of support services the student may need to achieve his or her best performance (that is, speech and language services, counseling, occupational therapy services)
- Determines the modifications that best fit the student's needs (changes or techniques that assist the student in learning, that is, extended time on tests, extra examples, having tests read aloud)
- Establishes the types of accommodations the student may need in order to assist him or her in school (that is, filters in fluorescent lights for a student with Crohn's disease, wider doors to accommodate wheelchairs)

Once these factors are determined, they are put together in the IEP document. It is this document that is developed, modified, and coordinated with parents and professionals who will be working with the student. As a result, a thorough understanding of the IEP process is a very important responsibility.

In this book we will take you through a step-by-step process of IEP development.

Purpose of an IEP

The IEP is a written record of the decisions reached by team members at the IEP meeting. The IEP serves many purposes:

- The IEP is the heart of IDEA 2004. It is a written statement that is developed, reviewed, and revised in an IEP meeting and serves as a communication vehicle between a parent and the school district.
- The IEP meeting serves as a communication vehicle between parents and school personnel and enables them, as equal participants, to jointly decide what the student's needs are, what services will be provided to meet those needs, and what outcomes may be anticipated.
- The IEP process provides an opportunity for resolving any differences between the parents and the agency over the special education needs of a student with a disability: first, through the IEP meeting, and second, if necessary, through the procedural protections that are available to the parents.

- The IEP sets forth in writing a commitment of resources necessary to enable a student with a disability to receive needed special education and **related services.**
- The IEP is a management tool that is used to ensure that each student with a disability is provided special education and related services appropriate to the student's special learning needs.
- The IEP is a compliance and monitoring document that may be used by authorized monitoring personnel from each governmental level to determine whether a student with a disability is actually receiving the free appropriate public education (FAPE) that the parents and the school have agreed to.
- The IEP serves as an evaluation device for use in determining the extent of the student's progress toward meeting the projected outcomes.
- The IEP defines and mandates an effective *process* that engages parents and school personnel in a meaningful discussion of the student's educational needs. The completed IEP should be the product of collaboration between parents and educators who, through full and equal participation, identify the unique needs of a student with a disability and plan the services to meet those needs.
- The IEP is not a performance contract or a guarantee by the district and the teacher that a student will progress at a specified rate. At the same time, the district must ensure that all services set forth in the student's IEP are provided, and it is also obligated to make good-faith efforts to assist the student in achieving his or her IEP goals and objectives.

The IEP can be more than an outline and management tool of the student's special education program. It should be an opportunity for parents and educators to work together as equal participants to identify the student's needs, what will be provided to meet those needs, and what the anticipated outcomes may be. It is a document that is revised as the needs of the student change. The IEP is a commitment in writing of the resources the school agrees to provide. Also, the periodic review of the IEP serves as an evaluation of the student's progress toward meeting the educational goals and objectives. Finally, the IEP serves as the focal point for clarifying issues and cooperative decision making by parents, the student, and school personnel in the best interests of the student. For all these reasons, the IEP is the cornerstone of special education.

13 Principles of IEP Collaboration

1. IDEA Emphasizes a Collaborative Approach

The IEP requirements under IDEA emphasize the importance of working cooperatively as a team. The law expects school districts to bring together parents, students, general educators, related service providers, and special educators to make important educational decisions for serving students with disabilities. With the combined knowledge and resources of these individuals, students will be assured greater support and subsequent success.

2. Parents Are Equal Partners in the Team Process

The team process should be a collaborative process between parents or guardians, school staff members, and other professionals. Parents have a unique and critically important perspective on their child's learning style, strengths, and needs. The school staff should ensure that parents feel welcomed and comfortable when communicating with school staff and at all meetings.

Parents have the right to be involved in meetings that discuss the identification, evaluation, IEP development, and educational placement of their child. The law ensures that parents and school personnel are equal partners in all steps during the team process.

Every effort should be made to resolve differences between parents and school staff through informal measures:

- Respect parents' right to disagree while looking for common goals and interests in a parent's requests and the school's position.
- Make sure you listen carefully to all proposals and understand the major issues.
- Brainstorm alternative solutions and offer reasonable compromises, keeping the needs of the student central to the discussions and the negotiated agreements.

The team should always work toward consensus. Nevertheless, school personnel ultimately have the responsibility to ensure that the IEP includes the services that the student needs. School districts are, by law, obligated to make a proposal to the parent. If agreement cannot be reached, the school district cannot delay in proposing the services that it believes are the best services to ensure that the student receives an effective education.

3. Student Participation Is Important and, at Times, Required

Students should also be considered important members of team meetings. As students get older, they should become more and more active within team meetings and advance their interests and preferences for determining the direction for the identified goals and services in the IEP. Supporting active student participation in the team process assists students in developing self-determination skills. Such skills are necessary in adult life.

School districts must explain to students their rights, including their right to attend team meetings and the importance of the corresponding responsibilities. Students are invited to attend from the age of 14—younger if the purpose of the meeting is to discuss transitional services. If the student does not attend the meeting, the district must take other steps to ensure that the student's preferences and interests are considered. For example, this would include individual meetings between the student and guidance counselors, staff, or school psychologists.

Some states decide when students are able to make their own decisions. For example, Massachusetts law establishes age 18 as the age of majority. At that age, students are adults and competent to make their own decisions, including decisions about special education services. Therefore, the school district at the student's 18th birthday and in the absence of any court action to the contrary must seek the consent of the student to continue the special education program. To prepare students for assuming their own decision making, teams must discuss the transfer of rights at least one year before students turn 18.

4. General Educators Play a Central Role

With all students accessing the general education curriculum, general educators are vital participants in the development, review, and revision of the IEP. As the experts on the general curriculum, their knowledge of the curriculum and how to modify the curriculum is vital to ensuring that a student participates in the general education environment and that the student makes progress in the general curriculum.

The general educator participates in the team if the student is or may be participating in the general education environment. Although the general educator may not need to stay for the entire team meeting or need to attend every team meeting, IDEA clearly includes general educators in the decision-making process.

5. IEP Development Is a Student-Driven Process

Once a student has been found eligible for special education services, an IEP must be developed. The IEP must address the unique needs of the student and, therefore, must be tailored to the individual student needs as determined during the evaluation. Good IEPs will be responsive to parents' concerns and the student's vision and will assist the student as much as possible in moving toward independence. The IEP is intended to be a useful document that helps educators to understand the student and how best to work with that student. In other words, the IEP should describe how the student learns, how the student best demonstrates that learning, and how the school staff and student will work together to help the student learn better. The IEP is not intended to be a daily, weekly, or monthly lesson plan but should provide a clear picture of the student's current abilities and needs and should identify key goals and objectives that provide a direction and focus for the student's learning over the next IEP period. If carefully and thoughtfully written, the IEP will serve as a vehicle for improving the educational experience and results for a student with disabilities. Although IEP development is a student-driven, individual process, there are some central concepts that the team should adhere to during a well-managed team meeting.

A well-managed team meeting will

- Obtain parent and student input
- Think about the student's future dreams and goals
- Understand how the student's disability(ies) affect the student's learning
- Know how the student performs today
- Address only the areas that are affected by the disability(ies)
- Provide a focus for the student's learning during the designated IEP period
- Reflect high expectations for the student
- Stay as close as appropriate to what the student's peers are learning and doing
- Identify supports and services the student needs for success

The IEP forms the basis for the placement decision. Therefore, the IEP must be developed in its entirety before placement is decided. The placement decision must be based on a careful reflection of the IEP, including the services that the team has identified as necessary and the impact of the disability on the student's learning. Finally, the team must be mindful of the requirements for placement in the least restrictive environment. Teams need to remember that removal from the classroom solely because of needed program modifications is not permissible (34 CFR 300.550(b)(2)). Only after the needs of the student and the types of services have been discussed by the team and agreed to in an IEP can the team effectively choose the placement.

6. The IEP Is Written to Fit the Student. The Placement Is Chosen to Fit the IEP.

The IEP under no circumstances should be written "to fit" a particular placement. Teams must remember this critical dictate when moving through the team process to ensure that the IEP is written to address the unique needs of the student.

7. Team Meetings Should Be Used as a Communication Vehicle

During an IEP meeting, team members share information and discuss the needs of the student. All members should listen carefully and share information that brings about a better understanding of the student. The discussion should connect one IEP element to the next and ensure internal consistency within the produced document. A team meeting works better if

- The meeting is small and focused on the student
- Its members are knowledgeable about the district, special education law, and the student
- Parents are respected participants, giving and receiving information that will assist everyone in making informed decisions

All team members should be treated as equal partners in the process. An atmosphere of mutual respect opens the lines of communication and builds a strong base for ongoing cooperation between parents, school district personnel, and other team members. School systems that routinely send evaluation reports to parents in advance of a meeting find that the team discussion is more focused and can immediately start with a common base of information rather than a lengthy recitation of evaluation results. This strategy allows for more time to brainstorm and to write the IEP itself. Parents then leave the meeting with a more solid understanding of their child and how the school system plans to help their child improve.

8. The IEP Is a Contract Between the School District and the Parent

The IEP should reflect the decisions made at the team meeting and should serve as a contract between the school system and parents. For that reason, the document must clearly communicate to parents the needs of their child, the steps the school district will take to address those needs, and the progress their child is expected to make during the period covered by the IEP at hand. The IEP must also be written in generally understandable language and free of educational jargon. The IEP does not serve as a guarantee of progress. Nevertheless, school districts must be aware that IDEA clearly states that a school district must make a good-faith effort to assist the student in making progress toward the IEP goals.

9. Each Team Meeting Is Unique

A team meeting is a group process and an individual inquiry process that makes no two team meetings alike as each group at each meeting considers what is best for each distinctive student. The team process will be affected by the differences among the individuals attending the meeting, by the differences among schools and school districts, by the differences among the types of evaluation data being considered, and by multiple other factors. Each group will arrive at different answers, ideas, and services to address a student's needs and will write the IEP in a different manner. All these differences should be expected and encouraged, as there is no single correct way to serve a student or to write an IEP. At times, team members are hesitant to make a recommendation for fear of setting a precedent. This fear is ungrounded, because no precedents can be set when the team responds to the unique and individual needs of an eligible student.

10. The IEP Should Serve to Focus the Special Education Services

The IEP will better serve the student if it focuses on what will make the biggest difference for that student and not on every aspect of every school day. The IEP should concentrate on offsetting or reducing the problems resulting from the student's disability that interfere with learning and educational performance. Therefore, team members need to narrow their focus as they discuss the contents of the IEP. The IEP elements in the opening pages of the document assist the team in developing a focused IEP.

11. Parents and Students Need to Give Input Into IEP Development

Parent and student input becomes the first indicator for defining the IEP focus. The placement of their input as the first order of business is deliberate and in keeping with the importance given to parent input in IDEA. Parents need to be asked to share their biggest concerns and their hopes for their child's accomplishments, as the parent's perspective is unique and important to the team's work. Parents, without exception, have a view of the student that cannot be duplicated by even experienced evaluators.

12. Teams Should Keep a Whole-Student Perspective

The team must next review the student's strengths, interests, personal attributes, and personal accomplishments as well as key evaluation results in order to keep a whole-student perspective when writing the IEP. Teams should avoid a segmented look at the student in which individual skills or problems are identified in isolation. The team will want to keep the big picture in mind and use the student's strengths to the best advantage in planning steps for the next IEP period. When developing an IEP for a student with an existing IEP, the team should always review the content of the existing IEP as they begin developing a new IEP. The new IEP should be revised and updated as needed to shift goals and services and to demonstrate a progression of learning. Each year's measurable annual goals should clearly show a step-by-step increase in a student's learning outcomes. Also, if necessary, any lack of expected progress needs to be discussed and addressed.

13. The Vision Statement Directs the Team's Attention Toward the Future

The vision statement focuses the team on the future of the student. The team steps back from the here and now to take a broader, long-range perspective as it looks to where this student is headed in the future. Developing the vision statement helps the team balance between the immediate concerns and the hopes and dreams for the future. Knowing where the student is headed makes it easier for the team to eventually determine what progress needs to be made this year. Teams must remember the ultimate goal for all students with disabilities is independence and productive lives. The team needs to look one to five years in the future—the timeline will depend on the student's age at the time of writing—when writing the vision statement. As the student becomes older and more involved in transition planning, the vision statement becomes the hopes and dreams of the student and not the parent and team. Also, the statement for older students must conform to federal regulations and be based on the student's preference and interests and include desired outcomes in adult living and postsecondary and work environments. For younger students, the team might want to project over a shorter span of time and concentrate on times when the student might be making a transition from preschool to elementary school, elementary school to middle school, or from a more restrictive environment to a less restrictive environment. For these younger students, the adults take the more active role in developing the vision statement.

2

IEP Preparation

Preparation Before the IEP Meeting

Several steps must be taken before a student can be considered for receiving special education and, if appropriate, related services (for example, occupational therapy or in-school counseling). Before organizing and planning an IEP meeting, make sure all the actions on the following checklist have been taken:

- Educators work with parents (and the student when appropriate) to try, and then evaluate, intervention methods geared to the concerns that led to the referral.
- Decide whether the student should be formally evaluated. Written consent from parents is required.
- Evaluate the student through a variety of assessments, observations, and information gathering, targeting all areas related to the suspected exceptionality.
- Have the **multidisciplinary team** (MDT, the team that performs the comprehensive assessment on a student with a suspected disability) examine the data and determine whether the student meets the criteria to be considered eligible for special education and, if appropriate, related services. Record determination results.

- Have the MDT determine whether the student has a **specific learning disability.** Record data and findings.
- Inform school and other personnel of the need for a meeting and schedule it for a time when every person needed is available. (Arrangements may need to be made to cover a class or relieve someone from a duty in order to attend.) Schedule the meeting to review the evaluation and determine the student's eligibility for services.
- Send a written notice to parents informing them of, and inviting them to, the meeting.
- Allow sufficient time for invitees to respond and have an opportunity to request another time in order to accommodate the parents' and educators' schedules.

Setting Up the IEP Meeting

Once all the legwork is done and the multidisciplinary team has determined that an IEP meeting is the next appropriate step for a student, the first consideration is to ensure that all the people who will make up the IEP team are aware of and have plenty of notice to make arrangements to be present. It is critical to plan carefully when and where the meeting should be held, whether it will be a continuation of the eligibility meeting or held separately a short time later. (The IEP meeting should be held within 30 days of the determination of eligibility.)

Parent participation at an IEP meeting is very important. Federal and state regulations require that efforts be made to afford parents the opportunity to participate. Many parents work, and thus, it is important to check with the parent whenever possible before considering the schedule of the IEP meeting to be definite. Being sensitive to parent needs and time limitations can foster the quality of parent participation. It is a good practice to give at least 10 days' notice of a meeting, although there are times when that may not be possible.

The school is often the best place to hold the IEP meeting. The staff should, nevertheless, be prepared with an alternative meeting place if the school site is not appropriate. In rural areas where parents may live long distances from the school, it might be necessary to consider other options, such as conference calls. In such cases, it is very important to ensure parents have full access to any material to which other members of the IEP team may refer during the meeting.

Giving Notice of an IEP Meeting

A phone conversation with a parent or a verbal invitation does not meet the requirement to notify parents of an IEP meeting. Federal and state regulations require that the parents of a student with a disability be provided with advance written notice of IEP meetings and any other meetings in which the parent has a right to participate in order to meet IDEA's definition of informed consent. If necessary, use certified mail or hand delivery to ensure that parents receive the notice.

Schedule the meeting at a time and place agreeable to the parents and the school.

The parents must also be afforded the opportunity to reschedule the meeting. The notice must tell the parents the purpose, time, and location of the meeting, inform them of who will be attending, and let them know that they may invite people to the meeting who have knowledge or special expertise about their child. They may also request a translator or interpreter, if needed.

When the student is 14 years old or older, or when transition services or planning will be discussed, the student also *must* be invited to his or her IEP meeting. At that time, it is necessary to provide a written invitation to the student also. While not all students are required to attend IEP meetings, it is desirable to invite the student to be part of his or her IEP team.

Note: There may be rare emergency situations in which an IEP meeting is needed and time does not permit a formal written notice. In such instances, documentation that notice was given via phone or face-to-face conversation with notes showing the notice requirements were met can replace the regular notification form or letter. Even in these circumstances, however, the notice must be given to the parents early enough to allow them an opportunity to attend or to reschedule the meeting if they are unable to attend.

Checklist Procedures for Notifying Parents of the IEP Meeting

The essential written notification of an IEP meeting (and students when appropriate) should be completed and delivered early enough so parents can plan to attend or request a change (a minimum of 10 days is suggested).

The notification letter should include the following:

- The name of each person expected to be attending the meeting
- The name and telephone number where the contact person (IEP coordinator or lead teacher) can be reached or where a message can be left

- A copy of the parental rights; this is mandatory
- If it is known that a parent will not be able to read or understand the notice, other ways to make the parent aware of the meeting and to give the parent an opportunity to review his or her rights should be considered, such as through a home visit or other personal contact.
- If it is known that English is not the primary language spoken at home, an interpreter to help deliver the notice should be arranged.
- The date the notice is sent or delivered and the method of delivery (e.g., hand-delivered, mailed) should be documented.

When an IEP Meeting Must Be Convened

An IEP meeting must be convened under the following circumstances:

- Within 30 days of determining a student eligible for special education and related services
- On or before the IEP annual review date
- When considering a change in the IEP (including placement)
- At the reasonable request of any IEP team member, including the parent, guardian, a person acting as a parent or surrogate parent, and the student's teacher
- To review or create an assessment plan to develop a behavior intervention plan in discipline matters related to suspensions or expulsions

An IEP is in effect for one year only. It is not appropriate to use an IEP amendment form to extend the duration of an IEP. IEP meetings should be scheduled well in advance of the annual review date to ensure that all IEPs are current.

Helping Students Prepare

Though the basic purpose of the IEP is the same for students of all ages, the law includes additional requirements and provisions for students age 14 and over. These students face transition into activities after leaving school, and their IEPs reflect the need for identifying realistic goals and developing skills to reach them. An important component of this process is the input of the student. Though the regulations require that students 14 and over be included in their IEP meetings, students of all ages would benefit from participating in the process, insofar as appropriate.

Self-advocacy is a learned skill for all students and a challenge for many. For individuals with exceptionalities, it is even more critical to be able to communicate their needs and interact with others in a way that can be understood and respected. Participating in the IEP process, at any age, gives the student a meaningful opportunity to begin to develop self-advocacy skills and the confidence to use them.

Even young students have a lot to say about themselves—their strengths, their needs, their interests and preferences, and what they would like to do in the future. A student's presence at IEP meetings reminds other team members that IEPs are opportunities for communication that focus on the student's abilities and interests. Students have much to gain from being involved in the IEP process.

The development of an IEP can be a positive learning experience when professionals and parents have a mutual respect for each other and value input from all team members. Preparing students for the meeting will help them feel comfortable enough to speak up regardless of who is present. Through participation, students are accepting responsibility, making informed decisions, communicating with adults, understanding their exceptionality, and making connections between current programs and future results.

Below is a list of activities that can be done by educators and parents to help a student prepare for his or her IEP meeting:

- Spend time allowing the student to think about what he or she wants from education.
- Fully explain the purpose of the IEP meeting and who will be present.

- Review the parts of the IEP and what each one means.
- Share information that others will have, such as the past IEP, and be sure the student understands what it says.
- Share with the student the kinds of conversations that might occur at the IEP meeting.

Characteristics of an Effective IEP Team Meeting

An effective meeting is characterized by clear goals, members feeling involved, voices being heard, opinions respected, concerns addressed, and a sense of accomplishment. The most important component of a meeting is the people in it. In an effective meeting, the group has an opportunity to give input and express views but remain positive and focused on the intended purpose and outcome. The facilitator takes the role of conductor at the meeting. Just like an orchestra conductor, he or she predetermines the program and directs the participants. The composing of a symphony takes effort, but the results are music, not spontaneous noise. Developing a quality IEP may take more than one meeting. Noise is spontaneous—it takes effort and planning ahead to create music!

There are things the facilitator can do to create an atmosphere that is conducive to harmonious interaction and keeps up a steady pace. Following are a few suggestions:

- Take time at the beginning of the meeting to get to know the participants. Through an informal (and unpressured) conversation, the facilitator may be able to get a sense of everyone's attitudes and concerns ahead of time and make them more comfortable.
- Gather extra resources that may be useful to explain or support educational findings or decisions, such as books, research, or other materials. The facilitator may ask specialists to help locate resources. Have these on hand for the meeting, if needed.
- Prepare a written agenda with time blocks in mind. For example, consider about how long it might take (with time for comments and questions) to go through each item on the IEP form. Allow a little extra time for unanticipated events. Keeping in mind that a meeting of this nature should not run more than 1.5 to 2 hours, the facilitator can then decide whether the objectives can be accomplished in one meeting, or whether two would be more reasonable.

- Check to be sure that the proposed meeting location has needed access and adequate space for each person expected at the meeting. The facilitator should ensure that participants are arranged so that no one is crowded or obscured and everyone has equal opportunity to see, hear, and be heard.
- Plan to create an open, welcoming atmosphere for the meeting by arranging to have pitchers of cold water on the table or a light snack provided. A small flower arrangement gives life to a room; or make the atmosphere more student-centered by adding some student-made art or decorations to the room.

The nature of an IEP meeting makes it special. Developing an IEP for a student shown to have exceptionalities often involves a mixture of people who have very different points of view and motivations, or even different cultures and languages. These strategies and ideas could apply to many kinds of meetings, but are particularly helpful and effective for use with IEP and other educational program meetings.

3

IEP Participants

IEP Team Members—
Roles and Responsibilities

Requirements for the Individualized
Education Program Team

> (B) **INDIVIDUALIZED EDUCATION PROGRAM TEAM**—The term "individualized education program team" or "IEP Team" means a group of individuals composed of—
>   (i) the parents of a student with a disability;
>   (ii) not less than one general education teacher of such student (if the student is, or may be, participating in the general education environment);
>   (iii) not less than one special education teacher, or where appropriate, not less than one special education provider of such student;
>   (iv) a representative of the local educational agency who—
>   (I) is qualified to provide, or supervise the provision of, specially designed instruction to meet the unique needs of students with disabilities;
>   (II) is knowledgeable about the general education curriculum; and
>   (III) is knowledgeable about the availability of resources of the local educational agency;

(Continued)

(Continued)

> *(v) an individual who can interpret the instructional implications of evaluation results, who may be a member of the team described in clauses (ii) through (vi);*
>
> *(vi) at the discretion of the parent or the agency, other individuals who have knowledge or special expertise regarding the student, including related services personnel as appropriate; and*
>
> *(vii) whenever appropriate, the student with a disability*

The next section will discuss in detail the roles and responsibilities of each member of the IEP Team.

The Parents of a Student With a Disability

> *The parents of a student with a disability are expected to be equal participants along with school personnel, in developing, reviewing, and revising the IEP for their student. This is an active role in which the parents*
>
> *(1) provide critical information regarding the strengths of the student and express their concerns for enhancing the education of their student;*
>
> *(2) participate in discussions about the student's need for special education and related services and supplementary aids and services; and (3) join with the other participants in deciding how the student will be involved and progress in the general curriculum and participate in State and district-wide assessments, and what services the agency will provide to the student and in what setting.*
>
> (64 Fed. Reg. 12,473 [March 12, 1999])

Parents are important team members who can

- Verify the accuracy of personal identifying information
- Provide information and observations about the level of the student's functioning in his or her home environment and community
- Provide information on the student's medical status

- Participate in developing educational goals and objectives based on the present level of academic achievement of functional performance and identified needs
- Participate in determining the special education and related services to be provided
- Participate in identifying an appropriate educational program for the student

Although parents are expected to be equal partners at the IEP meeting, writing IEPs or participating at IEP meetings is a new experience for many families. Information could be shared with parents throughout the evaluation process and prior to IEP notification about what will be discussed at the meeting, questions to consider, transition questionnaires, and so on. This would enhance parents' readiness to share their wishes (that is, goals) for their child, as well as to contribute to the determination of the student's needs and present levels of performance. Please remember that all information sent to parents must be in their **native language.** Districts must arrange for interpreters for parents when necessary.

Note: Although it is extremely desirable for parents to attend, a district cannot require parents to participate and some parents may choose not to participate. If the parents do not attend the IEP meeting, the district must provide prior written notice to the parents along with a copy of the initial or revised IEP. This notification should inform the parents that the IEP will be implemented 10 school days after the IEP meeting date unless the parents formally request a **due process** hearing.

Requirements For Parent Participation (Authority: 20 U.S.C. 1414 (d)(1)(B)(i) §300.345)

Parent participation.

(a) Public agency responsibility—general. Each public agency shall take steps to ensure that one or both of the parents of a student with a disability are present at each IEP meeting or are afforded the opportunity to participate, including—
(1) Notifying parents of the meeting early enough to ensure that they will have an opportunity to attend; and
(2) Scheduling the meeting at a mutually agreed on time and place.

(Continued)

(Continued)

(b) Information provided to parents.
  (1) The notice required under paragraph (a)(1) of this section must—
     (i)   Indicate the purpose, time, and location of the meeting and who will be in attendance; and
     (ii) Inform the parents of the provisions in §300.344(a)(6) and (c)(relating to the participation of other individuals on the IEP team who have knowledge or special expertise about the student).
  (2) For a student with a disability beginning at age 14, or younger, if appropriate, the notice must also—
     (i)   Indicate that a purpose of the meeting will be the development of a statement of the transition services needs of the student required in §300.347(b)(1); and
     (ii) Indicate that the agency will invite the student.
  (3) For a student with a disability beginning at age 16, or younger, if appropriate, the notice must—
     (i)   Indicate that a purpose of the meeting is the consideration of needed transition services for the student required in §300.347(b)(2);
     (ii) Indicate that the agency will invite the student; and
     (iii) Identify any other agency that will be invited to send a representative.

(c) Other methods to ensure parent participation. If neither parent can attend, the public agency shall use other methods to ensure parent participation, including individual or conference telephone calls.

(d) Conducting an IEP meeting without a parent in attendance. A meeting may be conducted without a parent in attendance if the public agency is unable to convince the parents that they should attend. In this case the public agency must have a record of its attempts to arrange a mutually agreed on time and place, such as—
  (1) Detailed records of telephone calls made or attempted and the results of those calls;
  (2) Copies of correspondence sent to the parents and any responses received; and
  (3) Detailed records of visits made to the parent's home or place of employment and the results of those visits.

(e) Use of interpreters or other action, as appropriate. The public agency shall take whatever action is necessary to ensure that the parent understands the proceedings at the IEP meeting, including arranging for an interpreter for parents with deafness or whose native language is other than English.

(f) Parent copy of student's IEP. The public agency shall give the parent a copy of the student's IEP at no cost to the parent.

Not Less Than One General Education Teacher of Such Student (If the Student Is, or May Be, Participating in the General Education Environment)

Very often, general education teachers play a central role in the education of students with disabilities, and they have important expertise in the general curriculum and the general education environment. Further, with the emphasis on involvement and progress in the general curriculum added by the IDEA, general education teachers have an increasingly critical role (together with special education and related services personnel) in implementing the program of free appropriate public education (FAPE) for most students with disabilities, as described in their IEPs (64 Fed. Reg. 12,472 [March 12, 1999]).

Thus, a general education teacher must, to the extent appropriate, participate in the development, review, and revision of the student's IEP, including assisting in (1) the determination of appropriate positive behavioral **interventions** and strategies for the student and (2) the determination of supplementary aids and services, program modifications, and supports for school personnel that will be provided for the student.

The teacher need not be required to participate in all decisions made as part of the meeting or to be present throughout the entire meeting or attend every meeting. (The appropriate length of the teacher's participation at a meeting will depend upon the student's needs and the purpose of that IEP team meeting.) For example, the general education teacher who is a member of the IEP team must participate in discussions and decisions about how to modify the general curriculum in the regular classroom to ensure the student's involvement and progress in the general curriculum and participation in the general education environment.

Specific circumstances, however, may make it unnecessary for the general education teacher to participate in discussions and decisions on, for example, the physical therapy needs of the student, if the teacher is not responsible for implementing that portion of the student's IEP.

In determining the extent of the general education teacher's participation at IEP meetings, public agencies and parents should discuss and try to reach agreement on whether the student's general education teacher who is a member of the IEP team should be present at a particular IEP meeting and, if so, for what period of time. The extent to which it would be appropriate for the general education teacher member of the IEP team to participate in IEP meetings must be decided case by case (64 Fed. Reg. 12,477 [March 12, 1999]).

Not Less Than One Special Education Teacher, or Where Appropriate, Not Fewer Than One Special Education Provider of Such Student

The special educator on the team can be either the student's special education teacher, or the student's special education service provider, such as a speech therapist, if the related service is considered specially designed instruction. If the student is being considered for special education for the first time, the role of the special education teacher could be filled by a teacher qualified to provide special education in the student's suspected area of disability. Occupational therapists, physical therapists, and guidance counselors cannot fill the role of the special education teacher or service provider on the IEP team, since these individuals do not provide specially designed instruction.

In deciding which teacher should participate, the district may wish to consider the following possibilities:

- For a student with a disability who is receiving special education, the teacher could be the student's special education teacher. If the student's disability is a speech impairment, the teacher could be the speech-language pathologist.
- For a student with a disability who is being considered for placement in special education, the teacher could be a teacher qualified to provide education in the type of program in which the student may be placed.

A Representative of the Local Educational Agency

The representative of the local educational agency (LEA) could be the special education director, a building principal, or another representative of the school district. Each district may determine what staff person will serve as its representative at a particular IEP meeting, as long as the person meets the following criteria:

(a) Is qualified to provide, or supervise the provision of, specially designed instruction to meet the unique needs of students with disabilities;

(b) is knowledgeable about the general curriculum; and

(c) is knowledgeable about the availability of resources of the public agency.

> . . . It is important, however, that the agency representative have the authority to commit agency resources and be able to ensure that whatever services are set out in the IEP will actually be provided. (64 Fed. Reg. 12,477 [March 12, 1999])

Since the decision about the type of program or services the student needs in order to attain his or her IEP goals is made at the IEP meeting, it is inappropriate to recess an IEP meeting because of a necessity to get an approval or decision from another administrator or policy maker who was not at the meeting on placement, services, or the amount of services. In most states, occupational therapists, physical therapists, school psychologists, social workers, guidance counselors, and adaptive physical education teachers cannot be the agency representative, since they are not qualified to provide or supervise the provision of specially designed instruction. The services they provide, such as counseling or physical therapy, are considered related services, not specially designed instruction. A special education teacher or a speech therapist could serve as the district representative, since, as teachers, they provide specially designed instruction, if they meet the other criteria.

An Individual Who Can Interpret the Instructional Implications of Evaluation Results

The individual who can interpret the instructional implications to decide may also be filling the role of general education teacher, special education teacher, LEA representative, or some other role of special expertise on the IEP team, as long as she or he can interpret the instructional implications of the evaluation results.

At the Discretion of the Parent or the Agency, Other Individuals Who Have Knowledge of or Special Expertise With the Student, Including Related Service Providers as Appropriate

> [T]he determination as to whether an individual has knowledge or special expertise . . . shall be made by the parent or public agency who has invited the individual to be a member of the IEP team. (64 Fed. Reg. 12,478 [March 12, 1999])

Whenever Appropriate, the Student With a Disability

If a purpose of an IEP meeting for a student with a disability will be the consideration of the student's transition service needs or needed transition services the . . . school district . . . must invite the student and, as part of the notification to the parents of the IEP meeting, inform the parents that the agency will invite the student to the IEP meeting.

If the student does not attend, the . . . school district . . . must take other steps to ensure that the student's preferences and interests are considered.

. . . Generally, a student with a disability should attend the IEP meeting if the parent decides that it is appropriate for the student to do so. If possible, the . . . school district . . . and parents should discuss the appropriateness of the student's participation before a decision is made, in order to help the parents determine whether or not the student's attendance would be (1) helpful in developing the IEP or (2) directly beneficial to the student or both. The . . . school district . . . should inform the parents before each IEP meeting . . . that they may invite the student to participate. (64 Fed. Reg. 12,473 [March 12, 1999])

Student participation in the IEP can be a significant step in assisting students to become their own advocates. As students prepare for the move from school to adult life, they will need opportunities to practice the skills necessary in situations where self-advocacy will be important.

Naturally, student participation is not accomplished by simply inviting the student to the IEP meeting. Student activities designed to engage the student in the IEP process to be a full participant in the meeting include

- Reviewing **assessment** information, especially career and vocational assessments, prior to the meeting
- Examining academic progress
- Participating in long-range planning
- Establishing goals in employment, education, independent living, and community participation
- Exploring postsecondary education and training programs
- Researching options available through adult service agencies
- Brainstorming strengths and needs
- Leading some of the discussion at the IEP meeting

Transition Services Participants and Providers

Any meeting to develop, review, or revise transition services in the IEP shall also include as participants

- A school district representative responsible for providing or supervising the provision of transition services
- Representatives of other participating agencies that are likely to be responsible for providing or paying for the transition services included in the student's IEP

> **Note:** When the participation of other agencies is deemed appropriate and an agency representative is unable to attend the meeting, the district should document its efforts to involve other participating agencies in the IEP meeting. Alternative means of participation in IEP meetings may be considered for agency representatives who are unable to physically attend a meeting because of distance or time constraints (that is, teleconference, written reports).

It is important to consider that the needs of the transitioning student will change with time. The IEP team configuration should reflect these changes.

When the student reaches age 14, the IEP team must begin the conversation about the student's long-range goals (that is, what the student expects to be doing after exiting public education) and how, through participation in a program of studies, the student will be prepared to reach those goals. While students may not have a specific career goal at age 14, it is important that he or she explore the options available and begin the goal-setting process.

The need to be prepared for such decision making is why early career exploration (visits to colleges, job shadowing, tours, project-based learning, etc.) is important in middle school and should continue in high school. Students at age 14 may not know what they would like to do after leaving school, but it is critical that they take the courses that will keep all likely options open to them. The IEP team becomes an important support in assisting the student in designing a program of studies that will allow the student access to postsecondary options. Researching and exploring these options become an important part of transition.

An IEP team may consider initiating transition planning before age 14 for students who may be **at risk** of dropping out or need assistance with drawing connections between learning and their desired goals when they leave school.

When the student reaches 16 years old, the IEP team must begin to formulate the links with postsecondary education, training, and adult services. Getting adult service agencies to attend IEP meetings may be difficult, but it is important for the LEA to establish and maintain communication with the agencies to ensure a smooth transition for students. Families and students also play an important role in this process by returning applications for adult services and keeping appointments.

The IDEA has specific steps an LEA must follow if an agency commits to services but does not follow through. The LEA must reconvene the IEP team and develop an alternative strategy to meet the student's needs.

When it is determined who will be at the meeting, the school district must notify parents at least 10 school days before the IEP meeting. The notice must indicate the purpose, time, and location of the meeting and who will be in attendance. The school district also must inform the parents of the right of the parents to invite other individuals who have knowledge or special expertise about the student, including related services personnel as appropriate, to be members of the IEP team.

It also may be appropriate for the agency to ask the parents to inform the agency of any individuals the parents will be bringing to the meeting. Parents are encouraged to let the agency know whom they intend to bring. Such cooperation can facilitate arrangements and help ensure a productive, student-centered meeting (64 Fed. Reg. 12,473 [March 12, 1999]).

Other Possible IEP Team Members

Representative of a Private School

If a student with a disability is enrolled in a private school and receives special education from the district, a representative of the private school must be invited to attend the IEP meeting. If the representative cannot attend, the district must use other methods to ensure participation by the private school, including individual or conference telephone calls.

After a student with a disability enters a private school or facility, any meetings to review and revise the student's IEP may be initiated and conducted by the private school facility at the discretion of the district.

If the private school or facility initiates and conducts these meetings, the district shall ensure that the parents and a district representative

- Are involved in any decision about the student's individualized education program
- Agree to any proposed changes in the program before those changes are implemented

Early Childhood Transition Providers

In the case of a student who was previously served under Part C, an invitation to the initial IEP meeting shall, at the request of the parent, be sent to the Part C service coordinator or other representatives of the Part C system to assist with the smooth transition of services (20 U.S.C. § 1414 (d) (1) (D)).

Related Service Personnel

If a student's evaluation indicates the need for a specific related service, the district should ensure that a qualified provider of that service attends the IEP meeting or provides a written report on the nature, frequency, and amount of related service to be provided to the student.

Other Individuals

At the discretion of the parent or district, other individuals who have knowledge of or special expertise with the student may be invited to the meeting (the determination of whether the person invited has such knowledge or special expertise is made by the inviting party, be it the parent or district). The district must inform the parents of their right to bring other participants to the meeting. It would be appropriate for the district to ask whether the parents intend to bring additional participants to the meeting.

It would not be appropriate for union representatives to attend IEP meetings because they would be acting in the interest of the teacher and not possess knowledge of or expertise with the student.

The attendance of attorneys at an IEP meeting is strongly discouraged because of the potential for creating an adversarial atmosphere that would not necessarily be in the best interests of the student.

Excusal of Team Members

A member of the IEP team shall not be required to attend an IEP meeting, in whole or in part, if the parent of a student with a disability and the local educational agency agree that the attendance of such member is not necessary because the member's area of the curriculum or related services is not being modified or discussed in the meeting (20 U.S.C. § 1414 (d) (1) (C) (i)).

A member of the IEP team may be excused from attending an IEP meeting, in whole or in part, when the meeting involves a modification to or discussion of the member's area of the curriculum or related services if:

1. *the parent and the LEA consent to the excusal; and*
2. *the member submits, in writing to the parent and the IEP team, input into the development of the IEP prior to the meeting (20 U.S.C. § 1414 (d) (1) (C) (ii)).*

A parent's agreement to the above shall be in writing (20 U.S.C. § 1414 (d) (1) (C) (iii)).

Questions and Answers About Other IEP Team-Related Topics

Can Anyone Represent Parents at an IEP Meeting?

A parent or guardian of a student with disabilities must be invited to attend all IEP meetings. If the student is a ward of the state, or parents or guardians cannot be located, the district must appoint a surrogate parent. If the student is a ward of the state, the student's parents must be given the opportunity to participate in the IEP meetings unless the parents' right to oversee the education of their child has been severed by the courts. Parents of a student who is a ward of the state may not sign as guardian. In this case, the district-appointed surrogate parent must be invited to the IEP meetings.

If a Student With a Disability Has Several General Education Teachers, Must All of Them Attend the IEP Meeting?

No. The IEP team need not include more than one general education teacher of the student. If the participation of more than one general education teacher would be beneficial to the student's success in school (e.g., to enhance the student's participation in the general curriculum), it would be appropriate for them to attend the meeting (64 Fed. Reg. 12,477 [March 12, 1999]).

> However, even if all the teachers do not participate, . . . the LEA is strongly encouraged to seek input from all the teachers who will not be attending. In addition, . . . the LEA must ensure that each general education teacher (as well as each special education teacher, related services provider, and other service provider) of an eligible student . . . (1) has

access to the student's IEP, and (2) is informed of his or her specific responsibilities related to implementing the IEP, and of the specific accommodations, modifications and supports that must be provided to the student. (64 Fed. Reg. 12,477–12,478 [March 12, 1999])

Even if a guidance counselor is certified as a general education teacher, she or he cannot fill the role of general education teacher at the IEP meeting. This role must be filled by the student's general education teacher.

If the Student With a Disability Is in a Substantially Separate Program or Does Not Have a General Education Teacher, Must a General Education Teacher Attend?

Yes, a general education teacher should participate as a member of the IEP team for a student with a disability who is in a substantially separate program. General education teachers are particularly familiar with the general education curriculum. Their presence helps ensure that the IEP team will consider the student's opportunity to be involved with and progress in the general curriculum. The general education teacher can provide valuable information on the specific curriculum areas to be addressed as well as modifications and accommodations that could be made for the student.

If a Student With a Disability Needs Related Services, Must a Related Service Provider Attend the IEP Meeting?

Although the regulations do not specifically require that the IEP team include related services personnel, it is appropriate for those persons to be included if a particular related service is to be discussed as part of the IEP meeting. . . . For example, if the student's evaluation indicates the need for a specific related service (e.g., physical therapy, occupational therapy, special transportation services, school social work services, school health services, or counseling), the . . . school district . . . should ensure that a qualified provider of that service either (1) attends the IEP meeting, or (2) provides a written recommendation concerning the nature, frequency, and amount of service to be provided to the student. This written recommendation could be part of the evaluation report. (64 Fed. Reg. 12,478 [March 12, 1999])

Can Parents or School Districts Bring Their Attorneys to IEP Meetings?

One may invite individuals to the IEP meeting if they have expertise or knowledge of the student that is pertinent to developing the IEP. If an attorney happens to have this type of relationship and wishes to contribute to the IEP process, such participation may be considered to be appropriate. Such a presence may, however, appear threatening to the other party and hinder the open atmosphere of sharing that is desirable at IEP meetings.

Section 300.344 (a)(6) authorizes the addition to the IEP team of other individuals at the discretion of the parent or the public agency only if those other individuals have knowledge or special expertise regarding the student. The determination of whether an attorney possesses knowledge or special expertise regarding the student would have to be made on a case-by-case basis by the parent or public agency inviting the attorney to be a member of the team.

The presence of the agency's attorney could contribute to the potentially adversarial atmosphere at the meeting. The same is true with regard to the presence of an attorney accompanying the parents at the IEP meeting. Even if the attorney possesses knowledge or special expertise regarding the student, . . . an attorney's presence would have the potential for creating an adversarial atmosphere that would not necessarily be in the best interests of the student.

Therefore, the attendance of attorneys at IEP meetings should be strongly discouraged. Further, . . . attorneys' fees may not be awarded relating to any meeting of the IEP team unless the meeting is convened as a result of an administrative proceeding or judicial action, or, at the discretion of the State, for a mediation conducted prior to the request for a due process hearing. (64 Fed. Reg. 12,478 [March 12, 1999])

4

IEP Team Meetings

The Team Process

Under IDEA, the IEP process is a focal point for reaching improved outcomes for students with disabilities. The process, critically important to students with disabilities, must be carefully managed to ensure that the unique needs of the student are addressed and to ensure full compliance with statutory and regulatory requirements.

The team has three important and integrated activities to manage. Each is of equal importance and interdependent on the quality of the other.

1. Eligibility determination: The team must first determine whether a student is eligible for special education services. This determination starts with the careful and thorough evaluation of the student in all areas of suspected disabilities.

2. Development of the IEP: Next, if the team has found the student eligible for special education, the elements of an individualized education program (IEP) must be discussed, planned, and then captured in a written document. Input from parents, the student, general educators, and special educators is necessary to complete this service contract, which sets high expectations for a student and then guides that student's special education services for the next year.

3. Placement decision. Once all the elements of the IEP are determined, including services and supports, a placement decision must be made. The first placement option considered for each student with a disability must be the general education classroom with the provision of needed aids and services. The law requires that students do not get placed outside the general education classroom unless their disability requires another setting. The team must always consider the unique needs of the student before making the final placement determination.

During the Meeting—Focused but Flexible

Even when all the initial steps are done and team members are assembled to begin, the IEP meeting will not run itself. One solution is to appoint a facilitator. This person's function is vital to ensuring that the goals of the meeting are met, the participants feel comfortable, and the time is used efficiently. The facilitator should have an agenda designed to accomplish the purpose of the meeting in the time allotted. During the meeting, the facilitator should keep the group focused on the agenda but be flexible enough to allow for the unexpected—perhaps some new information is revealed, a question raised, or a conflict arises. While offering everyone opportunities to communicate, the facilitator should keep the group focused on the positive and the present, rather than the negative and the past. The facilitator can remind the group that its common goal is to build upon the strengths of the student so that he or she may be as successful as possible.

The facilitator holds the key to the success of the meeting. He or she must conduct the meeting so that everyone stays on task yet has opportunities to contribute. Below are some tips on how to achieve this.

Strategies for Effective Meetings

- Have a prepared agenda. Either post it or give a copy to each participant.
- Thank all the participants for their time and interest.
- Open with something light and upbeat that helps relax the participants (but not a joke!).
- Remind participants that they are members of a team who all want the best for the student.
- Set the tone by defining the objectives for the meeting and what is to be accomplished.

- Encourage participants to introduce themselves and share their perceived role in the meeting.
- Pay attention to the time and keep the meeting moving.
- If the discussion gets off track, summarize what has been said and then redirect the topic.
- If a topic or issue arises that is not relevant to the IEP, place it on a sidebar as something that needs to be revisited. (Tip: List it on the board or a posted sheet of chart paper for all to see. At the end of the meeting, indicate how the topic or issue will be dealt with.)
- Use good listening skills to validate others' input and effective questioning techniques to encourage participation and stay on topic.

Guidelines for Running the IEP Meeting

Both the process and the product are important in the development of an IEP. This section includes information on the following components of the IEP process:

- Planning the meeting
- Conducting the meeting
- Concluding the meeting
- Follow-up after the meeting

Planning the Meeting

Identify Roles

- *Facilitator:* The person who keeps the meeting moving. The facilitator also ensures that everyone participates and that the discussion is publicly recorded on a writing surface.
- *Recorder:* The person who enters information on the IEP form.
- *Timekeeper:* The person who reminds participants of the meeting time frame.

Outline the Meeting Agenda

The written agenda should include statements such as

- Introduction of participants
- Discussion of evaluation data

- Discussion of each part of the IEP
- "What is the student doing now?" (PLEP)
- "What should the student be doing?" (goals and objectives or benchmarks)
- "How will we measure and report progress?"
- "What kind of services will the student need?"
- Discussion of placement
- Approximate length of the meeting (1 hour to 1 hour, 30 minutes)

Arrange for a Writing Surface

- Chalkboard, whiteboard, or large Post-it notes

Conducting the Meeting

Set the Stage

- Introduce the participants.
- Define the purpose of meeting.
- Provide an overview of the agenda and state the anticipated length of meeting.
- Announce a designated place to record issues for discussion at a later date.
- Inform parents of their right to request more time and a copy of the evaluation report.

Discuss Each IEP Element

Team discusses key questions listed under the heading Elements of the IEP:

- What is the student doing now? (PLEP)
- What should the student be doing? (goal)
- What will the student need to be able to do to achieve each goal? (objectives or benchmarks)
- How will progress toward goals be measured and reported?
- Are there special factors that need to be considered to allow the student to benefit from his or her education?
- Will the student participate in state and district assessments?
- What are the youth's transition service needs?
- What special education and other services are needed to meet the IEP goals? (summary of educational services)
- What is the most appropriate curriculum and environment to meet individual learning needs? (placement considerations)

Parents share information first.

- Educators acknowledge the family's efforts and respond to the family's views.
- Educators share additional information on the student's needs.
- Parents and educators confirm agreement.
- Team restates areas of agreement and discusses areas that are not in agreement.

When Appropriate, Discuss Transition

- Actively involve the youth and parents in the IEP meeting.
- Use the youth's strengths, needs, interests, and preferences to develop goals when schooling ends.
- At the latest, by the student's 14th birthday, develop a statement of transition service needs that specifies the courses of study that will lead to the youth's adulthood goals.
- At the latest, by the student's 16th birthday, develop a statement of needed transition services to achieve the youth's adulthood goals that is a coordinated set of activities and that includes instruction, related services, community experiences, employment, and other adult living objectives and also daily living skills and functional vocational evaluation if appropriate.
- Develop goals and objectives or benchmarks for the coordinated set of activities.
- Determine who will pay for the needed transition services.

Concluding the Meeting

- Briefly summarize the IEP discussion.
- Focus on a shared vision between parents and educators for working on goals at home and at school.
- Inform parents that the completed IEP document will be sent to them if the IEP has not been completed at the meeting.
- Inform parents that an IEP team meeting can be reconvened if they have concerns.

Follow-Up After the Meeting

- Complete the writing of all elements of the IEP and send it to parents if IEP writing was not completed at the meeting. Verify with the parents that the IEP accurately reflects what was discussed at the meeting.

- All the student's teachers—both special education and general education—related service personnel, and others who have the responsibility for implementing the student's IEP must be informed of their responsibilities. One way to do this is to give each person a copy of the student's IEP.

If transition has been discussed:

- Assist the youth and family by linking them to any needed adult services, supports, or programs.
- Reconvene the IEP meeting if goals are not being achieved, courses of study change, or if transition service needs are not being provided as planned.

5

Step-by-Step Development of the IEP

Step 1: Formulate a Statement of the Student's Present Level of Academic Achievement of Functional Performance

The IEP team reviews the existing evaluation data on the student, including information and concerns shared by the parents. The team also reviews any other current pertinent data related to the student's needs and unique characteristics, such as information provided by parents; progress toward desired outcomes for adult life; current classroom-based assessments; the most recent reevaluation; input from the student's special and general education teachers and service providers; and, as appropriate, the results of the student's performance on statewide and districtwide assessments. If an independent evaluation has been conducted, the results of that evaluation must also be considered if it meets the district's criteria for such evaluations. These results are summarized to describe the student's present levels of performance and educational needs.

Statements of the student's present level of academic achievement of functional performance in an area of need include how a student's disability affects his or her involvement and progress in the general education curriculum (that is, the same curriculum as for students without disabilities). For preschool students, present levels of performance describe how the disability affects the student's participation in age-appropriate activities. The IEP for every student with a disability, even those in separate classrooms or schools must address how the student will be involved and progress in the general education curriculum. The statement should accurately describe the effect of the student's disability on the student's performance in each area of education that is affected.

The following guidelines should be followed in developing the statement of the present level of academic achievement of functional performance.

- Statements should be written in easy-to-understand language that is free of educational jargon.
- Information must be current.
- Statements should reflect the results of the assessment data. Statements that relate scores to the student's level of functioning should accompany test scores. **Raw test scores** are not sufficient.
- There should be a direct relation between the present level of academic achievement of functional performance and the other components of the IEP. Thus, if the statement describes a problem with a student's reading, the reading problem should be addressed under both the goals and objectives and the specific special education and related services to be provided.

Section 300.347(a)(1) requires that the IEP for each student with a disability include *"a statement of the student's present levels of educational performance, including—(i) how the student's disability affects the student's involvement and progress in the general curriculum; or (ii) for preschool students, as appropriate, how the student's disability affects the student's participation in appropriate activities."* ("Appropriate activities" in this context refers to age-relevant developmental abilities or milestones that typically developing students of the same age would be performing or would have achieved.)

The IEP team's determination of how each student's disability affects the student's involvement and progress in the general curriculum is a primary consideration in the development of the student's IEP. In assessing students with disabilities, school districts may use a variety of assessment techniques to determine the extent to which these students can be involved in and progress in the general curriculum, such as **criterion-referenced tests, standardized achievement tests,** diagnostic tests, other tests, or any combination of the above.

The purpose of using such assessments is to determine the student's present levels of educational performance and areas of need arising from the student's disability so that approaches for ensuring the student's involvement and progress in the general curriculum and any needed adaptations or modifications to that curriculum can be identified.

Standardized test scores by themselves are not helpful in developing present levels of performance for the IEP because they do not provide material that is relevant to the regular classroom and specific enough to develop annual goals and short-term objectives. If, however, a team feels it is necessary to include test scores in describing a student's present level of educational performance, they should make sure that the results are self-explanatory or explained and ensure that the impact of the disability on the student's performance is stated. Also, in determining present levels, the IEP team should consider information and observations provided by the parents.

The results of performance-based statewide and districtwide assessments can be considered in developing present levels of performance, since there should be a clear link between these assessments and standards-based classroom instruction. They, too, should be coupled with day-to-day instructional and assessment information from the classroom as well as other sources of information. The present levels of performance should provide a basis for projecting goals and objectives that will be developed and help establish criteria for determining when the goals and objectives have been achieved. They should indicate what the student does or does not do in each area of concern at the time the IEP is developed. If the student uses assistive technology, performance data demonstrating its effect on performance is collected and may be noted in the IEP. Since, however, there is an area in the IEP specifically for documenting the supplementary aids, noting it for this statement is not required. It is from these specific levels that the participants at the IEP meeting can then develop annual goals and objectives that are relevant and then determine the supplementary aids and services and special education and related services that need to be provided for the student to meet the goals.

Present levels of performance statements should answer such questions as

- What are the student's unique needs that result from his or her disability?
- What is it that the student can and cannot do at this time?
- How do the student's unique needs affect the student's participation and progress in the general curriculum or, for a preschool student, participation in age-appropriate activities?

- What are the parents' concerns for the education of their child?
- What instructional and behavioral supports or services have been effective or ineffective in addressing the student's needs in the past year?
- What accommodations or program modifications or supplementary aids and services have been effective or ineffective in addressing the student's needs in the past year?
- What instructional supports and services will likely be supported and used by the student?
- What transition needs of the student must be addressed to prepare the student for living, learning, and working in the community as an adult?

In summary, present levels of performance should

- Be related to an area of need
- Describe performance in the general curriculum
- Describe what the student does (strengths) and needs to be able to do
- Be written in objective, measurable terms
- Omit test scores unless they are self-explanatory

Step 2: Determine the Four Need Areas

The following areas must be considered in reporting a student's present levels of performance and individual needs:

Academic and Educational Achievement and Learning Characteristics

- The student's current levels of knowledge and development in subject and skill areas, including, as appropriate
- Activities of daily living (e.g., personal care, preparing meals, household activities, managing resources)
- Level of intellectual functioning (e.g., general intelligence, attention, memory, problem-solving ability, language functioning)
- **Adaptive behavior** (e.g., the effectiveness with which the individual copes with the natural and social demands of his or her environment; how the student makes judgments and decisions)

- Expected rate of progress in acquiring skills and information (e.g., the pace at which a student learns new information or skills, in consideration of factors such as those associated with the student's levels of cognitive skills, interests, age, and history of rate of progress)
- Learning style (e.g., how the student learns best such as through visual or auditory **modalities,** hands-on approaches, cooperative learning, repetition)

Social Development

The degree and quality of the student's

- Relationships with peers and adults
- Feelings about self
- Social adjustment to school and community environment

Physical Development

The degree or quality of the student's

- Motor and sensory development
- Health
- Vitality
- Physical skills or limitations that pertain to the learning process

Management Needs

The nature and degree to which the following are required to enable the student to benefit from instruction:

- Environmental modifications (e.g., consistent room arrangement, materials and routine; written rules displayed; limited number of items on the student's desk)
- Human resources (e.g., a paraprofessional to assist the student to locate classes and follow schedules)
- Material resources (e.g., two sets of books—one for home and one for school; large print)

Management needs must be developed in accordance with the factors identified in the areas of academic or educational achievement and learning characteristics, social and physical development.

Sample

Present Levels of Performance and Individual Needs

Current functioning and individual needs in consideration of

- The results of the initial or most recent evaluation, the student's strengths, the concerns of the parents, the results of the student's performance on any state or districtwide assessment programs
- The student's needs related to communication, behavior, use of Braille, assistive technology, limited English proficiency
- How the student's disability affects involvement and progress in the general curriculum
- The student's needs as they relate to transition from school to activities when schooling ends (ages 14 and older)

Transcript Information—Secondary Students Only

- Diploma credits earned: 11
- Commencement-level state tests passed: Biology, Earth Science, Mathematics A, Global History
- Expected date of high school completion: 6/04

Academic and Educational Achievement and Learning Characteristics

Current levels of knowledge and development in subject and skill areas, including activities of daily living, level of intellectual functioning, adaptive behavior, expected rate of progress in acquiring skills and information, and learning style.

- Prior to his injury, Kevin was an honor student at the 10th-grade level and demonstrated particular strengths in mathematics and writing activities.

Strengths

- Current achievement testing shows he has maintained appropriate grade-level reading skills.
- Learns best when materials are presented visually. Still, he has some visual-perception problems (noted below).
- Is aware of the effects of his injury and has a positive attitude to overcoming them (based on student interviews and parent reports).
- Is open to trying different ways to compensate for his injuries but does not want to stand out as "different" among his peers.
- Does well when expectations are clearly and simply explained to him.
- Has retained prior learning in subject areas but has difficulty learning new information.

Written Expression

Testing and classroom assignments indicate difficulties with written expression:

- Omits punctuation and does not sequence sentences in a logical order in written work (topic sentence, supporting sentences, and conclusion).
- Written expression difficulties result in a slower pace of progress. (It takes him on the average twice as long as his peers to complete an assignment.)
- Writing difficulties also affect his ability to complete tests that require written expression within a prescribed time period.
- Has difficulty taking notes in class and understanding and benefiting from notes taken.

Mathematics Skills

- Achievement tests show basic computation skills are at appropriate grade level.
- In day-to-day class work, he has difficulty with problem-solving tasks that involve multiple steps (three or more).
- Unable to analyze the information presented in graphs and charts because of the level of detail and has difficulty separating object from background.
- Has retained the knowledge and skills necessary for maintaining a checkbook.

Organization Skills

- Has difficulty analyzing a task that has more than three steps (e.g., the steps to get ready for physical education class).
- Relies on following the actions of his peers but cannot follow teacher's directions independently when they involve multiple steps (more than three).

Memory and Attention

- Has difficulty remembering homework assignments and what books to bring to class, class schedule, and the combination to his locker. As a result, he misses an average of two classes per week and over a 30-day period he failed to complete 50 percent of his assignments.

Communication

- Has difficulty participating in oral discussions in the classroom, especially when new material is being taught, and he is having difficulty expressing new information.
- Answers direct questions appropriately, but when more than one topic is being discussed, he shifts unexpectedly from topic to topic, especially when he is not familiar with the subject being discussed.
- Speaks out of turn and responds inappropriately with contributions to conversations that are often off the topic.

Vocational Evaluation

- Interest inventories show preferences for work in agriculture, building, repairing, and working outdoors. Highest interest scores were in working with

(Continued)

(Continued)

plants and animals and tools and equipment. His assessed interests match his expresses vocational interests.

- Needs to develop strategies to address difficulties in comprehension, problem solving, new-task learning, staying on task, and endurance.

Social Development

The degree and quality of the student's relationships with peers and adults, feelings about self, and social adjustment to school and community environments

- Is a well-liked, cooperative student who has maintained close ties with his friends since the accident and continues his interest in sports activities.
- Responds to cues and seeks feedback from others in a positive manner.
- Enjoys and participates in individual school and community sports (e.g., swimming, racquetball).
- Has difficulty participating in team sports because he becomes very agitated when in a competitive situation.
- His self-awareness when speaking in front of his peers has resulted in his leaving class unexcused on the average twice a week.
- Needs to acquire the social and work skills that will enable him to get along with coworkers and respond appropriately to supervision.

Physical Development

The degree or quality of the student's motor and sensory development, health, vitality, and physical skills or limitations that pertain to the learning process

Health

- Experiences frequent fatigue throughout the day, especially after periods of reading and physical activity.
- Gets headaches at least once a week, which often necessitates trips to the nurse and result in frequent absences from class. If he remains in class, he often puts his head down and indicates he cannot concentrate.
- Needs to increase his level for work tolerance and endurance.
- Cannot participate in contact sports without medical clearance.

Sensory

- Hearing is within normal limits.
- Has visual perception problems in separating objects from background without strong contrast.

Management Needs

The nature of and degree to which environmental modifications and human or material resources are required to enable the student to benefit from instruction. Management needs are determined in accordance with the factors identified in the areas of academic and educational achievement and learning characteristics, social development, and physical development.

- Scheduled rest periods throughout the instructional day
- **Tasks analyzed** and written in steps
- Short and direct instructions
- Assistance during transition between classes
- Organizational strategies such as assignment notebooks, organizers
- Strategies to compensate for visual perception problems

Step 3: Consideration of Special Factors

The Law—The Individuals with Disabilities Education Improvement Act of 2004 (IDEIA)

(B) CONSIDERATION OF SPECIAL FACTORS—The IEP Team shall—

(i) in the case of a student whose behavior impedes the student's learning or that of others, consider the use of positive behavioral interventions and supports, and other strategies, to address that behavior;

(ii) in the case of a student with limited English proficiency, consider the language needs of the student as such needs relate to the student's IEP;

(iii) in the case of a student who is blind or visually impaired, provide for instruction in Braille and the use of Braille unless the IEP Team determines, after an evaluation of the student's reading and writing skills, needs, and appropriate reading and writing media (including an evaluation of the student's future needs for instruction in Braille or the use of Braille), that instruction in Braille or the use of Braille is not appropriate for the student;

(iv) consider the communication needs of the student, and in the case of a student who is deaf or hard of hearing, consider the student's language and communication needs, opportunities for direct communications with peers and professional personnel in the student's language and communication mode, academic level, and full range of needs, including opportunities for direct instruction in the student's language and communication mode; and

(v) consider whether the student needs assistive technology devices and services.

Explanation

As appropriate, the IEP team shall consider the following special factors and include statements addressing these needs in the student's IEP:

- If the student's behavior impedes his or her learning or that of others, the team shall consider, when appropriate, strategies such as positive behavioral interventions and supports to address that behavior.
- If the student has limited English proficiency, the IEP team shall consider the language needs of the student.
- If the student is blind or visually impaired, the IEP team shall provide for instruction in Braille and the use of Braille unless determined not to be appropriate for the student. This determination can be made only after an evaluation of the student's reading and writing skills, needs, and appropriate reading and writing media (including an evaluation of the student's future needs for instruction in Braille or the use of Braille).
- If the student is deaf or has a hearing impairment, the IEP team shall consider the language and communication needs of the student, opportunities for direct communication with peers and professional personnel in the student's language and communication mode, the student's academic level, and his or her full range of needs, including opportunities for direct instruction in the student's language and communication mode.
- If the IEP team determines that assistive technology devices (that is, electronic communication device, phonic ear) and services (that is, assistive technology evaluation, training, technical assistance) are necessary in order for the student to access and benefit from the educational program, such technology must be designated in the IEP.

The following information provides examples of guiding questions an IEP team may use to determine whether certain students need a particular device or service (including an intervention, accommodation, or other program modification) in order for the student to receive a free appropriate public education.

Are there special factors that need to be considered to allow the student to benefit from his or her education?

- Has the IEP team considered all the special factors without regard to disability category?
  - Behavior
  - Limited English proficiency
  - Communication
  - Assistive technology

- If the student is visually impaired, has the IEP team considered the student's need for Braille instruction?
- If the student is hearing impaired, has the IEP team considered
  - The student's language and communication needs?
  - Opportunities for direct communication with peers and school staff?
  - The student's academic level and full range of needs?

Special Factor 1: Students Who Demonstrate Behaviors That Impede Learning

A functional behavioral assessment (FBA) is conducted as part of an individual evaluation for each student with a disability who has behaviors that impede his or her learning or that of others. An FBA must also be conducted when disciplinary actions have resulted in the suspension or removal of the student from his or her current program for more than 10 days in a school year. An FBA provides information on why a student engages in a behavior, when the student is most likely to demonstrate the behavior, and situations in which the behavior is least likely to occur. The IEP of a student whose behavior impedes his or her learning or that of others must indicate the strategies, including positive behavioral interventions and supports, to address a student's behavior needs.

Key Question: Is the student's behavior affecting his or her learning or that of others?

The IEP team must identify strategies based on the results of the FBA, including positive behavioral interventions and supports to address those behaviors. When a student's behaviors are such that they are impeding learning, the IEP must identify, as appropriate, the student's present levels and needs, annual goals, including short-term objectives and benchmarks related to behaviors, and the special education and related services, supplementary aids, and services to be provided to the student, or on behalf of the student, any needed program modifications, and any supports for school personnel that are needed in order to address the behavior.

In determining the supports, services, interventions, or program modifications a student may need for addressing behaviors that impede learning, the IEP team should consider the following questions:

- What behaviors does the student exhibit that are different from those of same-age peers?
- When is the student most likely to exhibit the problem behavior?

- What are the general conditions under which the behavior usually occurs and probable consequences that serve to maintain it?
- What contextual factors (including cognitive and affective factors) contribute to the behavior?
- What specific events appear to be contributing to the student's problem behavior?
- What function(s) does the problem behavior serve for the student?
- What might the student be communicating through problem behavior?
- When is the student least likely to engage in the problem behavior?
- Does the student's behavior problem persist despite consistently implemented behavioral management strategies?
- Does the student's behavior place him or her or others at risk of harm or injury?
- Have the student's cultural norms been considered relative to the behavior in question?
- Do health-related issues affect the behavior?
- Does the student's disability affect his or her ability to control the behavior?
- Does the student's disability affect his or her understanding of the consequences of the behavior?
- What accommodations are necessary for instruction and testing?
- Does the student need an individual behavioral intervention plan?

Special Factor 2: Students With Limited English Proficiency

For all students with disabilities with limited English proficiency, the IEP team must consider how the student's language needs relate to the IEP. Schools must provide a student who have limited English proficiency with alternative language services to enable him or her to acquire proficiency in English and to provide him or her with meaningful access to the content of the educational curriculum that is available to all students, including special education and related services. The IEP team should consider the following questions:

Key Questions: Does the student's level of English language proficiency affect special education and related services the student needs? If so, to what extent?

Will the special education and related services that the student needs be provided in a language other than English?

- Has the student been assessed in English as well as in his or her native language?
- Did the evaluation of the student with limited English proficiency measure the extent to which the student has a disability and needs special education rather than measure the student's English language skills?
- Does the disability affect the student's involvement and progress in the bilingual education or English as a Second Language (ESL) program of the general curriculum?
- What language will be used for this student's instruction?
- What language or mode of communication will be used to address parents or family members of the student?
- What accommodations are necessary for instruction and testing?
- What other language services (that is, English as a second language, bilingual education) must be provided to ensure meaningful access to general and special education and related services?

Special Factor 3: Students With Visual Impairments

When a student is blind or visually impaired, the IEP team must provide instruction in Braille and the use of Braille unless the IEP team determines, after an evaluation of the student's reading and writing skills, needs, and appropriate reading and writing media, that instruction in Braille or the use of Braille is not appropriate for this student. The student's future needs for instruction in Braille or the use of Braille must also be considered. The IEP team should consider the following questions:

- Does the student have a disability in addition to blindness that would make using his or her hands difficult?
- Does the student have residual vision?
- Does the student use or need to learn to use assistive technology for reading and writing?
- Is the student's academic progress impeded by the current method of reading?
- Does the student use Braille, large print, recordings, or regular print?
- Will the student need to use Braille, large print, or recordings in the future?
- Have provisions been made to obtain in Braille the printed materials used by sighted students?
- Does the student need instruction in orientation and mobility?

- Does the student have appropriate listening skills?
- Does the student have age-appropriate social skills?
- What skills does the student need to enable him or her to learn effectively?
- What accommodations are necessary for instruction and testing?
- What is the potential loss of remaining vision?
- What is the amount of reading required of the student in the general education curriculum?
- Does the student have language-related learning disabilities?

Special Factor 4: Students With Communication Needs

The IEP team must consider the communication needs of the student, and in the case of a student who is deaf or hard of hearing, consider the student's language and communication needs. The IEP team must consider the student's opportunities for direct interaction with peers and educational personnel in the student's own language and communication mode. Opportunities for direct interaction (without needing an interpreter) in the student's own language and communication mode must also be described. The IEP team should consider the following questions:

Key Questions: Does the student need to learn or use special communication and language skills and strategies? If yes, do the student's annual goals and short-term objectives or benchmarks address affected areas?

- Does the student use American Sign Language?
- What mode of communication does the student use?
- What mode of communication does the family prefer?
- Is an interpreter or translator needed for the student to participate in and benefit from classroom instruction or interaction with peers and educational personnel?
- Does the student require assistive devices to facilitate the development and use of meaningful language or a mode of communication?
- Does the student require the use of hearing aids and assistive listening devices in order to maximize auditory training and language development in classrooms, related school activities, and at home?
- What environmental modifications are necessary to address communication needs?
- Are there opportunities for the student to participate in direct communication with peers and educational personnel?

- What opportunities exist for direct instruction (without an interpreter) in the student's language or mode of communication?

Special Factor 5: Students Who May Need Assistive Technology Devices and Services

Some students may require assistive technology devices and services to benefit from a free appropriate public education (FAPE). The IEP team must also consider whether the use of school-purchased assistive technology devices must be used in the student's home or in other settings in order

> **Key Question:** What, if any, assistive technology devices and services does the student need to achieve her or his annual goals, including benchmarks, or short-term objectives?

for the student to receive FAPE. Parental input in this area is especially important. The IEP team should consider the following questions:

- What can the student do now with and without assistive technology devices and services?
- What does the student need to be able to do?
- Can assistive technology devices and services facilitate student success in a less restrictive environment?
- Does the student need assistive technology devices and services to access the general curriculum or to participate in nonacademic and extracurricular activities?
- What assistive technology services would help the student participate in the general curriculum and classes?
- Does the student need assistive technology devices and services to benefit from educational or printed materials in alternative formats?
- Does the student need assistive technology devices and services to access auditory information?
- Does the student need assistive technology devices and services for written communication or computer access?
- Does the student need an assistive technology device or service for communication?
- Does the student need assistive technology devices to participate in statewide and districtwide testing?
- Will the student, staff, or parents need training to facilitate the student's use of the assistive technology devices?
- How can assistive technology devices and services be integrated into the student's program across settings such as work placements and for homework?

Step 4: Determination of Measurable Annual Goals (Including Academic and Functional Goals)

The term *individualized education program* or *IEP* means a written statement for each student with a disability that is developed, reviewed, and revised in accordance with IDEA and that includes

> *(II)   a statement of measurable annual goals, including academic and functional goals, designed to—*
>
> *(aa) meet the student's needs that result from the student's disability to enable the student to be involved in and make progress in the general education curriculum; and*
>
> *(bb) meet each of the student's other educational needs that result from the student's disability (IDEIA, 2004)*

Definition

Annual goals are statements that identify what knowledge, skills, and behaviors a student is expected to be able to demonstrate within the period of time from the time the IEP is implemented until the next scheduled review. Annual goals must be identified that meet the student's needs, as identified in the present levels of performance.

A goal is a measurable statement that describes what a student is reasonably expected to accomplish from the specialized educational program during the school year.

Explanation

> *The academic and functional goals should focus on the learning and behavioral problems resulting from the student's disability and be aligned with state and district performance standards. They should address the needs that are summarized in the statement of the student's present levels of academic achievement and functional performance. For those students taking alternate assessment, there should be at least one goal, with corresponding objectives or benchmarks, for each area of need.*
>
> *The goals and objectives or benchmarks provide a mechanism for determining whether the student is progressing in the special education program and the general education curriculum, and whether the placement and services are appropriate to meet the student's identified educational needs (IDEIA, 20 U.S.C. § 1414 (d) (1) (A) (i) (II)).*

Individual need determinations (that is, present levels of performance and individual needs) must provide the basis for written annual goals. The IEP must list measurable annual goals, consistent with the student's needs and abilities, to be followed during the period beginning with placement and ending with the next scheduled review by the team (effective dates of the IEP).

For each annual goal, the IEP must indicate the benchmarks and short-term instructional objectives and evaluative criteria, evaluation procedures, and schedules to be used to measure progress toward the annual goal.

The benchmarks or short-term instructional objectives must be measurable, intermediate steps between present levels of educational performance and the annual goals that are established for a student with a disability.

The measurable annual goals, including benchmarks or short-term objectives, must be related to

- Meeting the student's needs that result from the student's disability to enable the student to be involved in and progress in the general curriculum (or for preschool students, in appropriate activities)
- Meeting each of the student's other educational needs that result from the student's disability

Measurable annual goals set the general direction for instruction and assist in determining specific courses, experiences, and skills a student will need to reach his or her vision. Goals also are descriptions of what a student can reasonably be expected to accomplish within 1 school year. A goal must be meaningful, measurable, able to be monitored, and useful in decision making.

- The annual goal is meaningful if it specifies a level of performance and an expectation that is reasonable; the skill or knowledge the goal represents is necessary for success in school and lifelong activities; and the family believes the accomplishment of the goal is important.
- The goal is measurable if it reflects performance or behavior that can be measured or observed.
- A goal is able to be monitored it there are multiple increments in performance between the present levels of performance and the criteria stated in the goal. The goal should be written so that it can be monitored frequently.
- Finally, the goal is useful if it facilitates making decisions about the student's education and the effectiveness of the student's IEP.

To meet the requirements of this part, the IEP team reviews and analyzes the present levels of educational performance and then writes an applicable annual goal for each area of need described. Goals must be written so as to enable the student to be involved in and progress in the general curriculum and to advance in other areas of educational need.

The IEP team writes annual goals that

- Show a direct relationship to the present levels of educational performance
- Describe only what the student can reasonably be expected to accomplish within one school year or the 12-month term of the IEP
- Are written in measurable terms
- Prepare the student for his or her desired lifelong activities, when planning for the school-to-adult life transition

The goal must include at least three parts:

1. *Expected change in performance:* Specifies the anticipated change in performance from a baseline and usually reflects an action or can be directly observed

2. *Proposed area of change:* Identifies skill, knowledge, understanding, or behavior

3. *Proposed criteria:* Specify the amount of growth, how much and how frequent, or to what standard or level of proficiency

Principles of Formulating Goals for a Student's IEP

When formulating goal statements, use the following guidelines:

- Goals should be general statements that focus on deficit skill areas.
- Goals should be designed to address the needs identified in the statement of the student's present level of academic achievement of functional performance.
- Goals should be challenging and describe what a student can reasonably be expected to accomplish during the school year.
- All members of the IEP team should easily understand the language of the goals.
- Goals should be written to increase the student's successful participation in the general education curriculum and allow for

inclusion in the general education environment to the maximum extent appropriate, or for preschool students, to participate in appropriate activities with nondisabled peers.

Goals should be stated so they are meaningful. Helpful questions to ask include

- Is accomplishment of the goal necessary for success in current and future environments?
- Does the family believe the accomplishment of the goal is important?
- Does the goal specify a level of performance and expectation that is reasonable?
- Are the goals measurable; do they reflect behavior that can be measured?
- Are the goals written so they can be monitored frequently and repeatedly?
- Are the goals written to enhance decision making? Will monitoring the goal provide data that can be used to determine the effectiveness of the student's educational program?
- Do the goals reflect transition needs (if appropriate)?

Step-by-Step Procedures for Determining Measurable Annual Goals

Step A: Determine the Skills the Student Requires to Master the Content of the Curriculum

Annual goals should focus on the knowledge, skills, behaviors, and strategies to address the student's needs. A student's needs generally relate to domains such as reading, writing, listening, organization, study skills, communication, physical development, motor skills, cognitive processing, problem solving, social skills, play skills, memory, visual perception, auditory perception, attention, behavior, and career and community living skills. The goals on a student's IEP should relate to the student's need for specially designed instruction to address the student's disability needs and those needs that interfere with the student's ability to participate and progress in the general curriculum.

Goals should *not* be a restatement of the general education curriculum (that is, the same curriculum as for students without disabilities) or a list of everything the student is expected to learn in every curricular content area during the course of the school year or other areas not affected by the student's disability. In developing the IEP goals, the team needs to select goals to answer the question "What skills does the student require to master the content of the curriculum?" rather than "What curriculum content does the student need to master?"

For example, a student may be performing very poorly on written tests in global studies that require written expression. The IEP goal for this student should focus on developing written expressive skills (e.g., using outlines or other strategies to organize sentences in paragraphs) rather than the curriculum goal that the student will write an essay about the economy of a particular country. Generally, goals should address a student's unique needs across the content areas and should link to the standards so that a student has the foundation or precursor skills and strategies needed to access and progress in the curriculum.

Step B: How Far . . . by When?

From information in the present levels of performance, the team has identified which need areas must be addressed and where the student is currently functioning in each of those areas. The next step is to identify what the focus of special education instruction will be over the course of the upcoming year. The annual goals will guide instruction, serve as the basis to measure progress and report to parents and serve as the guideposts to determine whether the supports and services being provided to the student are appropriate and effective.

An annual goal indicates what the student is expected to be able to do by the end of the year in which the IEP is in effect (in other words, the period beginning with placement and ending with the next scheduled review by the team). The annual goal takes the student from his or her present level of performance to a level of performance expected by the end of the year.

To be measurable, an annual goal should, in language parents and educators can understand, describe the skill, behavior, or knowledge the student will demonstrate and the extent to which it will be demonstrated.

Examples: One year from now,

- Terry will ask questions about the instructions or materials presented to ensure comprehension.
- Tom will use a datebook for appointments and assignments.

- Brianna will stand at least two feet away from the other person while conversing.
- Lisa will walk ten feet independently.
- Mackenzie will speak in complete sentences.
- Ron will point independently to pictures described.
- Jose will use word prediction software to write essays.

Terms such as *will improve, will increase,* and *will decrease* are not specific enough to describe what it is the student is expected to be able to do in one year. To be measurable, a behavior must be observable or countable. In general, it is recommended that goals describe what the student will do, as opposed to what the student will not do.

Example:

- The student will ask for a break from work *versus* the student will not walk out of the classroom without permission.

Step C: Determine Short-Term Instructional Objectives

For each annual goal, the IEP must include short-term instructional objectives or benchmarks. The instructional objectives or benchmarks must include evaluative criteria, evaluation procedures, and schedules for measuring progress toward the annual goal. Short-term objectives and benchmarks should be general indicators of progress, not detailed instructional plans, that provide the basis for determining how well the student is progressing toward his or her annual goal and that serve as the basis for reporting to parents.

Generally, one annual goal would not include both short-term objectives and benchmarks. Whether short-term objectives or benchmarks are used for a particular annual goal is at the discretion of the team.

Short-term objectives are the intermediate knowledge and skills that must be learned in order for the student to reach the annual goal. Short-term objectives break down the skills or steps necessary to accomplish a goal into discrete components.

For example, the sequential steps that a student must demonstrate in order for him to reach the annual goal to "remain in his reading class for the entire period and ask for help when the reading work is difficult for him" are as follows:

- Grant will be able to identify what upset him after a behavioral disruption.

- Grant will be able to state the physical signs he is feeling when reading work gets difficult and leads to a behavioral disruption.
- Grant will raise his hand for assistance when he begins to experience those physical signs.

Step D: Determine Benchmarks

Benchmarks are the major milestones that the student will demonstrate that will lead to the annual goal. Benchmarks usually designate a target point in time for a behavior to occur (for example, the amount of progress the student is expected to make within specified segments of the year).

Generally, benchmarks establish expected performance levels that allow for regular checks of progress that coincide with the reporting periods for informing parents of their child's progress toward the annual goals. For example, benchmarks may be used for this same student for this annual goal as follows:

- By November, Grant will remain in his reading class for 15 minutes without disruptions.
- By February, Grant will remain in class for 25 minutes without disruptions.
- By April, Grant will remain in his reading class for 35 minutes without disruption.
- By June, Grant will remain in his reading class for 45 minutes without disruption.

Writing Short-Term Instructional Objectives and Benchmarks. The following template may assist in the writing of short-term objectives or benchmarks:

Student will (do what)—(to what extent)—(over what period of time) or (by when) as evaluated through _____ on the following schedule: _____.
   Examples:

- S. will wait his turn in group games for three to five turn-taking activities over three consecutive days as evaluated through teacher charting of the targeted behavior every four weeks.
- K. will highlight or underline important concepts in reading materials on four out of five trials over a two-week period as evaluated through corrected work in class every two months.

- By December, J. will initiate his classwork when prompted by the teacher within three minutes over ten consecutive trials as evaluated by structured observations of the targeted behavior once a month.
- L. will use appropriate phrases to request toys or activities during free play on five trials over a two-week period as evaluated by structured observations every eight weeks.
- D. will wait until all directions are received before beginning activities or assignments as evaluated through teacher charting of the targeted behavior every four weeks.
- By January, M. will independently remove himself from the situation on all occasions when he is teased by peers during recess as evaluated quarterly by daily self-monitoring checklists.

Short-Term Objectives or Benchmarks. The short-term objectives or benchmarks derive from the annual goals but represent smaller, more manageable learning tasks a student must master on the way to achieving the goals. The purpose of short-term objectives and benchmarks is to enable families, students, and teachers to monitor progress during the year and, if appropriate, revise the IEP consistently with the student's instructional needs. They describe how far the student is expected to progress toward the annual goal and by when. In most cases, at least two objectives or benchmarks should be written for each annual goal. Progress on each short-term objective or benchmark should be documented.

Short-term objectives generally break the skills described in the annual goal into discrete components. *Benchmarks* describe the amount of progress the student is expected to make in a specified segment of the year. Benchmarks establish expected performance levels that allow for regular checks of progress that coincide with the reporting periods for informing parents of their child's progress toward achieving the annual goals.

Objectives and benchmarks must be measurable; they must use language that will allow a **count** of what a student does (for example, "The student will write," "The student will read"). *Do not* use phrases such as "The student will understand" or "The student will appreciate").

Step E: Determine the Evaluative Criteria

Evaluative criteria identify how well and over what period of time the student must perform a behavior in order to consider it met.

How well a student does could be measured in terms such as

- Frequency (e.g., 9 out of 10 trials)
- Duration (e.g., for 20 minutes)
- Distance (e.g., 20 feet)
- Accuracy (90 percent accuracy)

The period of time a skill or behavior must occur could be measured in terms such as

- Number of days (e.g., over three consecutive days)
- Number of weeks (e.g., over a four-week period)
- Occasions (e.g., during mathematics and English classes, on six consecutive occasions)

Step F: Determine Evaluation Procedures to Measure the Student's Progress

Evaluation procedures identify the method that will be used to measure progress and determine whether the student has met the objective or benchmark. An evaluation procedure must provide an objective method in which the student's behavior will be measured or observed.

Examples: structured observations of targeted behavior in class; student self-monitoring checklist; written tests; audio-visual recordings; behavior charting; work samples.

Step G: Determine the Evaluation Schedules to Measure the Student's Progress

Evaluation schedules state the date or intervals of time by which evaluation procedures will be used to measure the student's progress toward the objective or benchmark. It is not a date by which the student must demonstrate mastery of the objective.

Examples: by March 2007, in three months, every four weeks, at the end of the term, quarterly.

Short-term objectives and benchmarks should include the following three components to ensure that they can be evaluated:

1. *Objective criteria* that enable progress to be monitored and allow for determination of the point at which the objective has been accomplished, such as

- 95 percent accurate
- Fewer than five times per day
- Fifty correct responses in one minute
- Four out of five trials correct on three consecutive days

2. *Evaluation procedures* to be used, such as
   - Written performance
   - Oral performance
   - Criterion-referenced tests
   - Parent report
   - Observation
   - Time sample
   - Teacher-made tests

3. *Schedules* to determine how often the objective will be measured, such as
   - One to two weeks
   - Twice a week
   - Once a month
   - Six weeks
   - Nine weeks
   - Each semester
   - Annually

Some examples of possible short-term objectives are given below. Each objective has numbers corresponding to the three components: (1) objective criteria, (2) evaluation procedure, and (3) schedules.

- To create (1) fewer than five disruptions per day for three consecutive days, (2) as observed and recorded by the teacher's paraprofessional, (3) each day.

Step H: Determine How Progress Toward Annual Goals Will Be Measured

In accordance with the procedures, methods, and schedules to measure a student's progress toward the annual goals, school personnel need to establish a reporting and recording system that ensures that a student's progress is objectively assessed. This information is necessary for reporting progress to parents and for the team to review the student's IEP.

FAQs About Annual Goals

For Each Identified Present Level of Performance, Must There Be Annual Goals?

Yes—For each identified present level of performance, there must be at least 1 annual goal specified. These goals and subsequent objectives form the basis for the curriculum and specially designed instruction provided to the student. They are, therefore, written in terms of what the student will achieve. They should not be written in terms of what a parent or service provider will provide to the student.

Annual goals state the anticipated achievement expected within a 12-month period of time, although they can be written for a shorter period. In developing annual goals, the present level of educational performance must be considered. Annual goals must not be a restatement of the present levels of performance. Yet anyone reviewing the IEP should be able to clearly determine the direct relationship between the two.

> Measurable annual goals, including benchmarks or short-term objectives, are critical to the strategic planning process used to develop and implement the IEP for each student with a disability. Once the IEP team has developed measurable annual goals for a student, the team (1) can develop strategies that will be most effective in realizing those goals and (2) must develop either measurable, intermediate steps (short term objectives) or major milestones (benchmarks) that will enable parents, students, and educators to monitor progress during the year, and if appropriate, to revise the IEP consistent with the student's instructional needs.
>
> The strong emphasis . . . on linking the educational program of students with disabilities to the general curriculum is reflected in 300.347(a)(2), which requires that the IEP include: a statement of measurable annual goals, including benchmarks or short term objectives, related to—(i) meeting the student's needs that result from the student's disability to enable the student to be involved in and progress in the general curriculum; and (ii) meeting each of the student's other educational needs that result from the student's disability. (64 Fed. Reg. 12,471 [March 12, 1999])

Must the Measurable Annual Goals Address All Areas of the General Curriculum or Only Those Areas in Which the Student's Involvement and Progress Are Affected by His or Her Disability?

Areas of the general curriculum that are not affected by the student's disability do not need to be specifically addressed in the IEP. Annual goals should address areas of the general curriculum that are directly affected by the student's disability. Accommodations and modifications may be needed for the student to participate in other areas of the general curriculum.

The school district . . . is not required to include in an IEP annual goals that relate to areas of the general curriculum in which the student's disability does not affect the student's ability to be involved in and progress in the general curriculum. If a student with a disability needs only modifications or accommodations in order to progress in an area of the general curriculum, the IEP does not need to include a goal for that area; however, the IEP would need to specify those modifications or accommodations.

School districts often require all students, including students with disabilities, to demonstrate mastery in a given area of the general curriculum before allowing them to progress to the next level or grade in that area. Thus, in order to ensure that each student with a disability can effectively demonstrate competencies in an applicable area of the general curriculum, it is important for the IEP team to consider the accommodations and modifications that the student needs to assist him or her in demonstrating progress in that area. (64 Fed. Reg. 12,472 [March 12, 1999])

What Are Short-Term Objectives or Benchmarks?

Short-term objectives or benchmarks are measurable, intermediate steps between an individual's present level of performance and the annual goal. Objectives should be based on a logical breakdown of the annual goal and reflect advancement toward that goal. They therefore must be provided for each area in which present levels of performance and annual goals have been stated.

Each annual goal must include either short-term objectives or benchmarks. The purpose of both is to enable a student's teacher(s), parents and others involved in developing and implementing the student's IEP, to gauge, at intermediate times during the year, how well the student is progressing toward achievement of the annual goal. IEP teams may continue to develop short-term instructional objectives, that generally break the skills described in the annual goal down into discrete components. The revised statute and regulations also provide that, as an alternative, IEP teams may develop benchmarks, which can be thought of as describing the amount of progress the student is expected to make within specified segments of the year. Generally, benchmarks establish expected performance levels that allow for regular checks of progress that coincide with the reporting periods for informing parents of their child's progress toward achieving the annual goals.

An IEP team may use either short term objectives or benchmarks or a combination of the two depending on the nature of the annual goals and needs of the student. (64 Fed. Reg. 12,476 [March 12, 1999])

Can Short-Term Objectives or Benchmarks Be Changed Without Initiating Another IEP Meeting?

If either a parent or the school district believes that a required component of the student's IEP should be changed, the school district must conduct an IEP meeting if it believes that a change in the IEP may be necessary. (64 Fed. Reg. 12,471 [March 12, 1999])

Since short-term objectives, benchmarks, and annual goals are required components of the IEP, a meeting must be held with all required team members if any of these are going to be changed. The team will then make the needed changes in the IEP and thus a new IEP will have been developed. IDEA allows no such thing as an addendum to an IEP.

Sample

**Measurable Annual Goals and
Short-Term Instructional Objectives and Benchmarks**

Annual Goal: Kevin will accurately interpret graphs and charts to solve grade-level mathematical problems.

Instructional Objectives or Benchmarks	Evaluation		
	Criteria	Procedures	Schedule
Kevin will use manipulatives to reproduce graphs and charts to solve math problems.	4–5 times over 2 weeks	Classroom assignments Tests	Every 4 weeks
Kevin will highlight the large print graphs and charts to increase the contrast between the various parts of the graph, in order to solve math problems.	4–5 times over 2 weeks	Classroom assignments Tests	Every 4 weeks
Kevin will orally describe the material presented on graphs and charts to the teacher, in order to solve the problem.	4–5 times over 2 weeks	Classroom assignments Tests	Every 4 weeks

Annual Goal: Kevin will use graphic organizers to write a three-paragraph essay using correct sequencing of sentences including topic sentence, supporting sentences, and conclusion.

Instructional Objectives or Benchmarks	Evaluation		
	Criteria	Procedures	Schedule
Kevin will use graphic organizers to write a three-sentence paragraph using correct sequencing of sentences including topic sentence, supporting sentences, and conclusion with assistance by November.	5 times over 2 weeks	Writing sample Tests Classroom assignments	Every 6 weeks
Kevin will use graphic organizers to write a five-sentence paragraph using correct sequencing of sentences including topic sentence, supporting sentences, and conclusion with assistance by January.	4–5 times over 2 weeks	Writing sample Teacher observation Classroom assignments	Every 6 weeks
Kevin will use graphic organizers to write a two-paragraph essay using correct sequencing of sentences including topic sentence, supporting sentences, and conclusion without assistance by March.	4–5 times over 2 weeks	Writing sample Teacher observation	Every 6 weeks
Kevin will use graphic organizers to write a three-paragraph essay using correct sequencing of sentences including topic sentence, supporting sentences, and conclusion without assistance by June.	4–5 times over 2 weeks	Writing sample Tests Classroom assignments	Every 6 weeks

Step 5: Reporting Progress
Toward the Annual Goals to Parents

Requirements

The IEP must provide a statement of how the student's parents will be regularly informed of their child's progress toward the annual goals and the extent to which that progress is sufficient to enable the student to achieve the goals by the end of the year. The frequency with which parents are informed must be at least as often as parents of nondisabled students are informed of their children's progress.

What Is the Purpose of Reporting Progress to Parents?

Regular reports to parents provide a mechanism to monitor a student's progress toward the annual goals and to evaluate the effectiveness of the student's special education services. The process of assessing, evaluating, and reporting student progress enables the school and the parents to monitor student learning and identify what action, if any, is needed to help a student succeed. If progress is such that the student is not expected to reach his or her annual goals, the team should review and, if appropriate, revise the student's IEP to ensure that the student is being provided the appropriate supports and services.

What Should Be Included in the Progress Report?

The report of the student's progress must, at a minimum, inform parents of

- Their child's progress toward the annual goals
- Whether this progress is sufficient for their child to achieve the goals by the end of the school year

The objectives and benchmarks provide the steps toward the annual goals and establish the criteria, schedule, and method for evaluating the student's progress. Establishing goals that are measurable is important so that progress can be adequately assessed. To report student progress, the teachers must have gathered evidence of what students are able to do in each annual goal area. Establishing a systematic data **collection** system is the very first step to effective progress reporting to parents.

How Should Progress Be Reported?

The method or combination of methods to inform the parents of their child's progress is left to local discretion. The unique needs of the students determines the manner selected to inform parents and might vary from student to student.

There are many ways a student's parents can be informed of their child's progress, including periodic parent-teacher conferences, written progress reports, and student-parent-teacher conferences, among other methods. The reports to the parents do not need to be lengthy or burdensome, but they need to be informative. For example, the report to parents could include a statement of the goals with a written report of where the student is currently functioning in that goal area or a rating of progress to indicate whether the student's progress to date will likely result in the student reaching the goal by the end of the year. The progress report to parents should be in addition to the student's regular report cards that provide grades for courses or subject areas.

Sample

Reporting Progress to Parents

Annual Goal: Kevin will use graphic organizers to write a three-paragraph essay using correct sequencing of sentences including topic sentence, supporting sentences, and conclusion.

1st period ending November	2nd period ending January	3rd period ending March	4th period ending June	July–August
Kevin is writing three-sentence paragraphs with correct sequencing, including a topic sentence, supporting sentence, and conclusion. Objective met.	Kevin needs assistance to develop the outline, but once developed, he follows it to accurately write a five-sentence paragraph using a graphic organizer.	Kevin is writing two-paragraph essays when following a written outline.	Kevin independently develops a graphic organizer (outline) and writes three-sentence paragraphs using correct sequencing of sentences.	

How Often Must Progress Be Reported?

Progress must be reported at least as often as progress is reported to parents of students without disabilities. The IEP could indicate frequency of reporting, for example, as

- Monthly
- Quarterly
- At the end of each term
- At three-month intervals

Sample

Reporting Progress to Parents

The student's progress toward the annual goals and the extent to which the progress is sufficient to enable the student to achieve the goals will be reported to parents as follows:

Manner	Frequency
Written progress reports on IEP goals	Every three months
Parent-teacher conferences	Four times per year

Step 6: Determine the Extent to Which the Student Will *Not* Be Able to Participate in General Education Programs (LRE Explanation)

Definition

The IEP must include a statement of the extent, if any, to which the student will not participate in the general education classroom, general education curriculum, extracurricular, or other nonacademic activities. The same program options and nonacademic services that are available to students without disabilities must be available to students with disabilities. Program options typically include art, music, industrial arts, clubs, home economics, sports, field trips, and vocational education. Nonacademic services and

Note: If modifications (supplementary aids and services) to the general education program are necessary to ensure the student's participation in that program, those modifications must be described in the student's IEP.

extracurricular activities typically include athletics, health services, recreational activities, and special interest groups or clubs.

Explanation

Section 300.347 (a) (4) requires that each student's IEP include "An explanation of the extent, if any, to which the student will not participate with nondisabled students in the regular class and in [extracurricular and other nonacademic] activities." This is consistent with the least restrictive environment (LRE) provisions at Secs. 300.550–300.553, which include requirements that

- Each student with a disability be educated with nondisabled students to the maximum extent appropriate (Sec. 300.550 (b) (1))
- Each student with a disability be removed from the general educational environment only when the nature or severity of the student's disability is such that education in regular classes with the use of supplementary aids and services cannot be achieved satisfactorily (Sec. 300.550 (b) (1))
- To the maximum extent appropriate to the student's needs, each student with a disability participates with nondisabled students in nonacademic and extracurricular services and activities (Sec. 300.553)

All services and educational placements under Part B of IDEA 2004 must be individually determined in light of each student's unique abilities and needs to reasonably promote the student's educational success. Placing students with disabilities in this manner should enable each disabled student to meet high expectations in the future.

Although Part B requires that a student with a disability not be removed from the general educational environment if the student's education can be achieved satisfactorily in regular classes with the use of supplementary aids and services, Part B's LRE principle is intended to ensure that a student with a disability is served in a setting where the student can be educated successfully. Even though IDEA does not mandate regular class placement for every disabled student, IDEA presumes that the first placement option considered for each disabled student by the student's placement team, which must include the parent, is the school the student would attend if not disabled, with appropriate supplementary aids and services to facilitate such placement. Thus, before a disabled student can be placed outside the general educational environment, the team must consider the full range of supplementary aids and services that, if provided, would facilitate the student's placement in the regular classroom setting.

After that consideration, if the team determines that a particular disabled student cannot be educated satisfactorily in the general educational environment, even with the provision of appropriate supplementary aids and services, that student then could be placed in a setting other than the regular classroom. Later, if it becomes apparent that the student's IEP can be carried out in a less restrictive setting, with the provision of appropriate supplementary aids and services, if needed, Part B would require that the student's placement be changed from the more restrictive setting to a less restrictive setting.

In all cases, placement decisions must be individually determined on the basis of each student's abilities and needs, and not solely on factors such as category of disability, significance of disability, availability of special education and related services, configuration of the service delivery system, availability of space, or administrative convenience. Rather, each student's IEP forms the basis for the placement decision.

Further, a student need not fail in the regular classroom before another placement can be considered. Conversely, IDEA does not require that a student demonstrate achievement of a specific performance level as a prerequisite for placement into a regular classroom.

To meet the requirement of this component, the IEP team should review and analyze

- Special education and related services
- Supplementary aids and services
- Where the services will be provided
- How frequently the services will be provided

The IEP team *writes* an explanation of the extent, if any, to which the student will *not* participate with nondisabled students in the general education classes and in extracurricular and other nonacademic activities. The explanation must be consistent with the following provisions for the least restrictive environment:

- Each student with a disability must be educated with nondisabled students to the maximum extent appropriate
- Each student with a disability will be removed from the general education class only when the nature or severity of the student's disability is such that education in general education classes

with the use of supplementary aids and services cannot be achieved satisfactorily

- To the maximum extent appropriate, each student with a disability participates with nondisabled students in nonacademic and extracurricular services and activities

Step 7: Determine Placement Options

Justification for Placement

The IEP team must provide a written justification for their decision to place a student in any setting outside the regular classroom. Removal from the general educational classroom shall occur only when the nature or severity of the student's needs is such that education in regular classes with the use of supplementary aids and services cannot be achieved satisfactorily.

The IEP team must provide a written description of the options considered and the reasons those options were rejected for *each* placement alternative considered for the student. The IEP team must then provide a written description of the option accepted and reasons the option was accepted. **In addition, the team must discuss the *potential harmful effects* of the accepted special education placement.** Written descriptions are *not* required for rejecting options in the continuum that are more restrictive than the ones accepted by the IEP team.

Acceptable justifications might include the following (or a combination of the following):

- It completely supports the information in all parts of the IEP.
- It includes references to the use of supplementary aids and services and explains why each was rejected.
- It considers the student's educational history and individual evaluation information.
- It clearly outlines group discussion and serious consideration.
- It goes beyond description of a preferred option such as "student needs better ratio than this option can provide" and tells why this is essential to student's unique learning needs and describes those needs.

Unacceptable justifications:

- The justification given is a *non*academic reason.
- The justification given is a *non*individualized reason.

- The option chosen reflects an administrative convenience.
- The option chosen reflects a decision based on a disability category.
- The justification given is identical to the one given for all other students in that placement.
- The justification given is based on the availability of related services.
- The justification given is based on the availability of services.
- The justification given is based on availability of space.
- The justification given is based on availability of particular curriculum content or method of curriculum delivery.
- The justification given has no written documentation.
- The justification given is based on configuration of services.
- The option chosen does not reflect alternative aids or services tried or examined.
- The justification given is based on absence of an appropriate continuum of currently available placements.
- The justification given consists of considerations, conditions, or documentation analyzed prior to or independent of the student's IEP.

Examples of a Justification Statement

Example #1:

LRE and General Education:

- The regular class: Sally demonstrates a severe reading deficit when compared to her peers, which necessitates specialized individualized instruction that is not available in the regular class.
- Extracurricular and nonacademic activities: She has access to all extracurricular and nonacademic activities.
- Her LEA home school: The programs and services that meet her needs are not offered in her home school.

Example #2:

LRE and General Education:

- The regular class: Severe reading deficits necessitate small-group individualized instruction.
- Extracurricular and nonacademic activities: She fully participates with her peers.
- Her LEA home school: She is attending her home school.

Special Education Program and Services

The IEP must specify the special education program or services needed by the student. Special education programs and services include

- Special classes
- Resource rooms
- Direct and indirect consultant teacher services
- Travel training
- Home instruction
- Special teachers, including itinerant teachers

There are additional special education programs and services (e.g., transitional support services, assistive technology services, and transition services) that will be documented in other sections of the IEP.

In recommending special education services for a preschool student, the Committee on Preschool Education must first consider the appropriateness of providing (1) related services only or (2) special education itinerant services only or (3) related services in combination with special education itinerant services or (4) a half-day preschool program or (5) a full-day program.

Special Education Itinerant Teacher (SEIT)

For preschool students, SEIT services have the purpose of providing special individualized or group instruction or indirect services. Indirect SEIT services means consultation with a certified special education teacher who assists the student's teacher in adjusting the learning environment or modifying the teacher's instructional methods to meet the student's individual needs. SEIT services may be provided to a preschool student with a disability who attends an early childhood program (or with documented medical or special needs, SEIT may be provided in the student's home). Recommendations for SEIT services should specify whether the service will be provided individually or for a group.

Consultant Teacher Services

Consultant teacher services are defined as direct and indirect services provided to a school-age student with a disability who attends general education classes, including career and technical education classes or to such student's general education teachers or both.

- Direct consultant teacher services means specially designed individualized or group instruction provided by a certified special education teacher to a student with a disability to help the student benefit from the student's general education classes.
- Indirect consultant teacher services means consultation with a certified special education teacher who assists the general education teacher in adjusting the learning environment or modifying instructional methods to meet the individual needs of a student with a disability who attends the general education teacher's classes.

If the student's IEP indicates consultant teacher services, the IEP *must* specify the general education class(es) (including career or technical education classes, as appropriate) where the student will receive the services.

A student could receive both direct and indirect consultant teacher services. It is recommended that the IEP specify the type of consultant teacher services the student will receive (that is, direct or indirect) so that it is clear to parents and educators the extent to which such services will be provided. If indirect consultant teacher services are to be provided, the IEP must indicate the general education class being taught by the teacher receiving the consultation (the IEP might read, for example, "Consultant teacher—indirect for English").

The effective implementation of this service requires general and special education teachers to work cooperatively to address the needs of students with disabilities. After the development of an IEP in which consultant teacher services are recommended, the general education teachers of the student for whom the service will be provided must be given the opportunity to participate in the instructional planning process with the consultant teacher to discuss the objectives and to determine the methods and schedules for such services.

Resource Room Program

A resource room program is a special education program for a student with a disability who needs *specialized supplementary instruction* (that is, instruction in addition to the student's general education instruction) in an individual or small-group setting for a portion of the school day. As examples, a resource room program might be recommended for students who need specialized supplementary instruction in organization skills, reading, the use of an assistive technology device, the use of Braille, or the use of a compensatory strategy.

Special Class

Special class means an instructional group consisting of students with disabilities who have been grouped together because of similar individual needs for the purpose of receiving specially designed instruction. A special class may be provided as a separate class or as a class within a general education class.

If the student's IEP indicates a special class will be provided, the IEP must describe the special class size. Special class size is defined as the maximum number of students who can receive instruction together in a special class and the number of teachers and paraprofessionals assigned to the special class (e.g., six students to one teacher and one paraprofessional). For preschool students, the IEP must also indicate whether the special class is a half-day or a full-day program.

Travel Training

Travel training is a special education service that means providing instruction, as appropriate, to students with significant cognitive disabilities and any other students with disabilities who require this instruction to enable them to develop an awareness of the environment in which they live and learn the skills to move effectively and safely from place to place within that environment (e.g., in school, in the home, at work, and in the community).

Adapted Physical Education

Adapted physical education means a specially designed program of developmental activities, games, sports, and rhythms suited to the interests, capacities, and limitations of students with disabilities who may not safely or successfully engage in unrestricted participation in the activities of the general physical education program.

Sample

Recommended Special Education Programs

Special Education Programs and Services	Frequency	Duration	Location	Initiation Date
Resource Room	5 times per week	40 minutes	Resource room	1/14/06
Consultant teacher (direct)	3 times per week	40 minutes	English class	1/14/06

Step 8: Determine Related Services

The Law

> *(26) RELATED SERVICES—*
> *(A) IN GENERAL—The term "related services" means transportation, and such developmental, corrective, and other supportive services (including speech-language pathology and audiology services, interpreting services, psychological services, physical and occupational therapy, recreation, including therapeutic recreation, social work services, school nurse services designed to enable a student with a disability to receive a free appropriate public education as described in the individualized education program of the student, counseling services, including rehabilitation counseling, orientation and mobility services, and medical services, except that such medical services shall be for diagnostic and evaluation purposes only) as may be required to assist a student with a disability to benefit from special education, and includes the early identification and assessment of disabling conditions in students.*
> *(B) EXCEPTION—The term does not include a medical device that is surgically implanted, or the replacement of such device.*

Related services means developmental, corrective, and other supportive services as required to assist a student with a disability. The IEP must indicate the specific related services, if any, that the student needs and must be based on the individual student's need for the service. The IEP should specify whether the services will be provided in individual or small-group sessions. Related services may include the following services, among others:

- Speech and language pathology
- Audiology services

- Psychological services
- Counseling services
- Physical therapy
- Orientation and mobility services
- Parent counseling and training
- School health services
- School social work
- Assistive technology services
- Rehabilitation counseling
- Occupational therapy

The above list of related services is not meant to be complete but is rather a list of the most common related services. With that in mind, IEP teams may identify other related services necessary to help a student benefit from special education. The school district must provide these services.

> *The list of related services is not exhaustive and may include other developmental, corrective, or supportive services if they are required to assist a student with a disability to benefit from special education. This could, depending upon the unique needs of a student, include such services as nutritional services or service coordination. These determinations must be made on an individual basis by each student's IEP team.* (64 Fed. Reg. 12,479 [March 12, 1999])

Determine Special Transportation Needs

The IEP must specify any special transportation, including any appropriate special transportation equipment (such as special or adapted buses, lifts, and ramps), that is needed by the student as a consequence of the unique needs related to the student's disability for

- Traveling to and from school (including such school-related programs as work programs and settings other than the school where the student receives education or special education services)
- Traveling in and around the school

In developing its recommendation for a preschool student with a disability, the Committee on Preschool Education (CPSE) must identify transportation options for the student and encourage parents to transport their child at public expense where cost-effective. The

IEP must indicate how the preschool student will be transported to his or her special education program (e.g., parent transportation or transportation arranged by the county).

Determine Frequency, Duration, and Location of Related Services

The Total Amount of Service Required by the Student per Week

The amount of service to be provided must be stated in the IEP so that the level of the agency's commitment of resources will be clear to parents and other IEP team members. The amount of services may be stated as a range (e.g., 45–60 minutes) only if the IEP team determines that a range is necessary to meet the unique needs of the student (e.g., services needed only when a seizure occurs). A range may not be used because of personnel shortages or uncertainty about the availability of staff.

As long as there is no change in the overall amount per week, some adjustments in scheduling the services should be possible (based on the professional judgment of the service provider) without holding another IEP meeting.

The Frequency of On-Site Program Review by Each Itinerant Service Provider

For example, if a student receives daily speech services from a paraprofessional or from a teacher who does not hold an endorsement in speech and language pathology, monthly on-site supervision of the student's speech services by a certified speech language pathologist is required. Both the amount of daily service and the amount of program supervision by the certified speech pathologist must be listed on the IEP. Examples of complying with the above requirements are listed below:

- Reading services, 60 minutes per day, 5 days per week.
- Physical therapy services, 60 minutes per week.
- Itinerant speech therapy supervision provided by a speech language pathologist, 120 minutes per month.
- Speech—language therapy—assistive technology (electronic communication device), 30 minutes per week.

The Amount and Frequency of Program Supervision by Certified Special Education Staff

When a staff person who is not certified in special education provides special education or related services (that is, a paraprofessional or general education teacher), the IEP must clearly document the amount and frequency of program supervision by the certified special education staff. The special education teacher or related service provider is responsible for designing the program and services provided.

The Amount and Frequency of Counseling Services

Counseling services provided by qualified social workers, psychologists, guidance counselors, or other qualified personnel must be clearly documented in the IEP. If the IEP team determines the counseling services to be necessary but the services are provided by an agency other than the school district, those services must also be listed on the IEP.

> **Note:** Individually prescribed devices such as glasses or hearing aids are generally considered to be personal items and are not a service to be provided by the district and thus would not be listed as a service need on the IEP.

Projected Starting Date and Anticipated Frequency, Duration, and Location of Services

The projected starting date and anticipated frequency, duration, and location of services (and modifications) must be indicated for each special education and related service. The date must include the month, day, and year and extend no more than a year from the date of the meeting. The location refers to the type of environment that is the appropriate place for the provision of the service (e.g., the regular classroom, resource room). The total time that a student with a disability spends receiving general education, special education, and related services should equal the total amount of time the student spends in school.

Sample

Recommended Related Services

Related Services	Frequency	Duration	Location	Initiation Date
Speech and Language Therapy—group	2 times per week	30 minutes	Therapy room	10/14/02
Counseling—individual	1 time per week	30 minutes	Counselor's office	10/14/02
Job Coach—individual	1 time per week	120 minutes	Job site	1/3/03

Step 9: Determine Program Modifications, Accommodations, Supplementary Aids, and Services

The Law

(33) SUPPLEMENTARY AIDS AND SERVICES—The term "supplementary aids and services" means aids, services, and other supports that are provided in general education classes or other education-related settings to enable students with disabilities to be educated with nondisabled students to the maximum extent appropriate in accordance with section 612(a)(5).

Supplementary aids and services and/or program modifications or supports means aids, services and other supports that are provided in general education classes or other education-related settings to enable students with disabilities to be educated with nondisabled students to the maximum extent appropriate in the least restrictive environment. The IEP must specify the projected date for initiation of services and the frequency, location and duration of such services.

Accommodations mean the provisions made to allow a student to access and demonstrate learning. Accommodations do not substantially change the instructional level, the content, or the performance criteria but are made in order to provide a student equal access to learning and equal opportunity to demonstrate what is known. Accommodations shall not alter the content of the test or provide inappropriate assistance to the student within the context of the test.

Accommodations change how students learn and the ways they demonstrate what they have learned. The students are working on the same instructional objectives and content as the other students.

Modifications are substantial changes in what a student is expected to learn and demonstrate. Changes may be made in the instructional level, the content, or the performance criteria. Such changes are made to provide a student with meaningful and productive learning experiences, environments, and assessments that are based on individual needs and abilities.

Modifications imply a change in the type and amount of work expected of the students. For example, a student may be working on a lower level than the other students in the class. In some instances, the student may be working on a skill related to that upon which other students are focusing.

Following are examples of supplementary aids and services, accommodations, and program modifications:

- A note taker
- Instructional materials in alternative formats (e.g., Braille, large print, books on tape)
- Extra time to go between classes
- Special seating arrangements
- Highlighted work
- Study guide outlines of key concepts
- Use of a study carrel for independent work
- Assignment of paraprofessional staff
- Behavior management and support plan
- Extra time to complete assignments

Modifications and Accommodations of Environment

Assign Preferential Seating

The teacher will place the student's desk in the best area in the classroom for the student to participate and learn. An example would be at the front of the class so that he or she can see the board better.

Alter the Physical Room Environment

The teacher will arrange the classroom furniture, temperature, and lighting to enhance the student's ability to concentrate and learn.

Use Learning Centers

A learning center is usually a section of the classroom where the teacher has established an independent student activity that usually reinforces a concept that the teacher has taught. The center can be set up for any content area. Students can work at the center independently, with another individual, or in small groups.

Use Notebook for Assignments, Materials, and Homework

Designate a notebook as the place where the student writes his or her assignments, scheduled tests, or special materials needed for each class. The student does not use the notebook for anything else. The student's teacher can initial the assignments to indicate the information is correct, and the parent can initial that he or she saw the assignments.

Provide Individualized or Small Group Instruction

The teacher will work with the student on a one-to-one basis or in small groups with a maximum of eight students.

Assign Peer Tutors, Work Buddies, and Note Takers

Peer tutoring is when the teacher assigns a student who has mastered needed skills to work with another student who needs help in learning the same skills. Work buddies are students who are paired to work together on an assignment or a task, and a note taker is a student who is selected to take notes that will be copied for another student who is unable to take his or her own notes.

Reduce or Minimize Distractions

The teacher will make alterations to the classroom or to the student's assigned seat so that distractions are reduced to a minimum. Examples would be to cover the window on the door to the classroom to restrict the view of activities in the hall and to limit the number of distracting items decorating the classroom walls. Another possibility is to limit the number of materials on the student's desk.

Consider Alternative Grouping

The teacher will group students into small groups according to like needs or instructional focus.

Stand Near the Student When Giving Directions

The teacher will move close to the student when telling the student how to do a task or when telling the student how to correct a problem to assure the student's attention.

Provide Adaptive Equipment

If a student needs special equipment to be able to perform a task, it will be provided. Examples: a magnifying glass to better see words on a page, batteries for an assistive listening device, probes to use the computer, and special chairs.

Modifications and Accommodations of Teaching Strategies

Teach to Student's Learning Style

The teacher will modify instruction and materials to address the student's strongest learning style.

- *Visual:* The student learns best by seeing the material or task to be learned.
- *Tactile:* The student learns best by touching the material to be learned.
- *Auditory:* The student learns best by hearing the material or task to be learned.
- *Kinesthetic:* The student learns best by doing or moving.
- *Multisensory:* The student learns best by seeing, hearing, touching, and performing the task to be learned.

Provide Individualized or Small Group Instruction and Testing

The teacher will teach or test the student on a one-to-one basis or in a group with a maximum of eight students.

Use Cooperative Learning Strategies

The teacher will assign students to teams who work together on a task or a project. Each student has a specific task or responsibility. The teacher provides the team with feedback for desired academic outcomes and positive behavior.

Modify Assignments as Needed

The teacher will make changes in the requirements of certain tasks. Examples: The student may be given more time to complete an assignment. The number of problems and questions may be reduced. The number of paragraphs required in a paper may be reduced. The student may give an oral report rather than a written paper.

Break Tasks and Procedures Into Sequential Steps

The teacher will divide tasks into the necessary steps for completion. The student will perform one step at a time until the task is completed.

Use Strategies for Mastery and Overlearning

The task to be learned is taught until the student can perform it automatically.

Teach Concrete Concepts Before Teaching Abstract Concepts

The teacher will use objects or pictures to teach a concept that the student can see and touch before teaching abstract concepts.

Limit the Number of Concepts to Be Introduced at One Time

Concepts that are presented to the student will be limited to one or two at a time, according to the student's ability to understand.

Utilize Oral Responses to Assignments and Tests

The student will be given the opportunity to answer questions on an assignment or test orally rather than in writing. A scribe (usually the teacher or paraprofessional) records the student's oral answers.

Read Class Materials Orally

The teacher or a student will read the material presented in class aloud.

Provide Practice Activities and Immediate Feedback

The student is given immediate feedback while he or she learns new skills.

Outline Notes and Key Sections of the Text to Emphasize the Main Idea

The student, teacher, or another student will prepare an outline of assigned reading that highlights the main ideas. Highlight pens or tape may be used.

Use Hand-On Activities and Manipulatives

The student learns a task by doing it, or by touching and moving concrete objects to perform the task required.

Use Verbal and Visual Cues to Reinforce Instruction

Students are taught by using words or picture associations. The teacher may also use visual cues to prompt a student to use a learned strategy or technique.

Provide Options for Students to Obtain Information and Demonstrate Knowledge Through the Use of

- *Tape recorders:* The student tapes lectures or explanations.
- *Word processors:* The student uses a word processor or computer to complete written assignments.
- *Calculators:* The student uses a calculator for computation.
- *Interviews:* The student answers orally or interviews others to obtain necessary information.
- *Alternative projects:* If an assigned project requires more or different skills than the student possesses, he or she may be given another project that he or she can complete.
- *Oral reports:* The student orally reports on information acquired rather than in writing.

Teach Students to Use Strategies Such as

- *Preview, review, and predict:* The student looks over the material to be read, reviews the material, and thinks ahead and predicts what is going to happen.
- *Ask and answer:* The student asks questions as new material is being presented or read. After answering the questions, the teacher checks for accuracy and understanding.
- *Summarize and synthesize:* The student summarizes a large amount of information, stating the main ideas and essential details. The student will then express this information in his or her own words.
- *Provide opportunities for generalization of skills:* The teacher will create opportunities for the student to use newly acquired skills in a variety of settings and situations. Examples: using new behavior skills in the library or on the playground; using safety skills outside the school building; using reading skills in another class or in the library.

Modifications and Accommodations of Materials

Shorten Assignments

The teacher will reduce the number of questions to be answered, pages to be read, sentences to be written, or problems to be solved.

Use Text, Workbooks, and Worksheets at a Modified Reading Level

The teacher will select materials that cover the content to be taught but are written at the student's reading level.

Provide Learning Materials to Supplement Instruction

The teacher will assist the student in acquiring content material by providing materials that address each student's learning styles or processing need. The materials may be visual, auditory, tactile, kinesthetic, or any combination of the above. They may also be a simplified version of other materials.

Alter the Format of Materials on a Page

The material given to the student can be changed by using special type, by highlighting certain words, or by the way the material is spaced on the page. The material can be larger than normal or can have certain words or phrases in bold print or underlined. The page may have more white space than typical worksheets.

Modify, Repeat, and Model the Directions

The teacher will change the directions for a specific assignment; the teacher may repeat the directions until the student understands what to do; the teacher may demonstrate for the student how to perform the required task.

Utilize Large Print, Braille, or Recorded Books

The student may be provided with books that have large print or books that have been Brailled, or books that have been tape-recorded.

Color-Code Materials

Materials are color-coded so that the student can find the materials easily and organize classes and assignments. Specific content can be highlighted in an assignment or other written materials to cue the student. Examples:

English texts and folders may be green and spelling may be yellow; a student's belongings might be color-coded so that he or she knows that the materials with blue dots are his or hers; place values and computation signs in math might be color-coded to remind the student of what to do.

Transferred Answers

When an assignment or a test is presented in such a way that the student cannot write on the test or the page presented, the student will use another sheet of paper or a computer to answer questions. The teacher or paraprofessional will copy the student's answers on the paper to be turned in.

Modifications and Accommodations of Time Demands

Increase the Amount of Time Allowed to Complete Assignments and Tests

The teacher gives the student more time to finish assignments and to take tests.

Limit the Amount of Work Required or the Length of Tests

The teacher will reduce the size of the assignments or reduce the number of questions on tests.

Allow Breaks During Work Periods or Between Tasks

The teacher will schedule or allow breaks for the student while working on assignments and between tasks.

Provide Cues and Prepare for Transitions in Daily Activities

The teacher will tell the student when it is time to change activities by using methods such as ringing a bell, using a musical tone, pointing to a picture or written schedule, getting out specific materials, or using verbal cues.

Modifications and Accommodations for Behavior Concerns

Assure Curriculum Is Appropriate and Needed Modifications Have Been Implemented

The teacher will provide materials that are age-appropriate and are written at the student's functional level. A behavior management and support plan addressing the student's specific behavior concerns should be implemented in all the student's classes.

Provide Instruction in Social Skills

The teacher will write daily lesson plans that include instruction of skills that address the social deficits of the student.

Reinforce Appropriate Behavior

When the student exhibits appropriate behavior, the teacher, paraprofessional, or person in charge should **reinforce** that behavior with a **positive** comment, gesture, or reward.

Determine the Reason for a Behavior and Teach Replacement Skills

The teacher or IEP team should determine the reason for the student's behavior through the use of a functional behavior assessment. Once the purpose for the behavior has been determined, the teacher should teach the student a replacement behavior that is appropriate and that will result in an outcome that meets the student's needs.

Establish Procedures and Routines to Assist the Student in Completing Activities

The teacher will establish guidelines and routines for the student that will make it easier and be in the best interest of the student to complete assigned tasks.

Conduct a Problem-Solving Session That Focuses on the Specific Issue

The teacher will involve the students in a discussion of an issue that presents a problem to the class or the school. Open discussion would take place on the issue and ways to solve it. Together the group would select the best way to solve the problem and implement the solution.

Offer a Systematic Program to Increase Self-Esteem

The teacher will establish a program with daily and weekly activities designed to assist students in recognizing their strengths and feeling better about themselves. These activities are included in the teacher's lesson plans.

Conduct Student-Teacher Conferences

The student and teacher would sit down together to discuss problems and to reach an agreement on how the problem could be solved.

Modify the Student's Schedule

If the student is exhibiting inappropriate behavior as a result of being in a classroom where he or she is being bullied or harassed or is with other students who have too much influence over the student's behaviors, his or her schedule of classes could be changed to eliminate some of the problem behavior. The schedule might also be changed to match the student's time of alertness or to place him or her in a classroom with a teacher who is better able to meet his or her needs.

Use Token Economy Reinforcement Strategies

The student is given a token when he or she exhibits appropriate behavior. The tokens are exchanged at a later date for something more valuable to the student.

Use a Structured Individualized Behavior Management Plan That Emphasizes Positive Reinforcement Techniques

A structured individualized behavior management plan is a plan written for a specific student to address his or her behavior problems. The purpose of the plan is to get the student to exhibit the desired behavior and to reward him or her when he or she exhibits the desired behavior.

Sample

Program Modifications, Accommodations, and Supplementary Aids and Services

Program Modifications, Accommodations, and Supplementary Aids and Services	Frequency	Duration	Location	Initiation Date
Use of graphic organizers for writing assignments	Daily	Writing assignments	English class History class	10/14/02
Extended time for writing assignments	Daily	Writing assignments	English class History class	10/14/02
Scheduled rest periods for fatigue	Daily every 2 hours	20 minutes	Nurse's office	10/14/02
Presentation of curricula content organized into smaller parts	Daily	New lessons	All academic classes	10/14/02
Teacher provided notes or outlines of unit information	Once a week	New lessons and units	All academic classes	10/14/02

Other: Assignment notebook; written schedule to assist Kevin to transition from class to class.

Determine Test Accommodations

The IEP must indicate the needed individual testing accommodations, if any, to be used consistently by the student:

- In his or her recommended education program
- In the administration of districtwide assessments of student achievement

Examples of test modifications follow.

Use of Scribe or Tape Recorder

Unless the IEP waives spelling, punctuation, and paragraphing requirements, the student must provide all information, including spelling of difficult words, punctuation, paragraphing, grammar, and similar usual requirements of the task when using a scribe or tape recorder.

- Scribes must record word-for-word what the student dictates or records, leaving out punctuation and capitalization and circling all words that are difficult to spell.
- Lined paper should be used and the scribe should write on every other line.
- When dictation and tape transcription is completed, the scribe should ask the student to spell aloud any difficult words and the scribe should write the student's spelling above the circled words. Difficult words are words at or above the grade level of the test.
- For capitalization, punctuation, and spelling tasks, the scribe shows the student the written response and asks him or her to indicate where capitalization, punctuation, and paragraphing should be used.
- The student reads the completed dictation and transcription and indicates whether there are any further changes to be scribed on the skipped lines.
- The scribe must then transfer the student's completed response into the test booklet and staple the student's dictation to the test booklet.

The accommodation "use of scribe" generally necessitates an alternate location and extended time in order for its implementation to be workable. These additional accommodations must also be specified on the IEP. If "extended time" and "separate location" are needed only when the use of a scribe is required, that must be indicated so that the accommodations are not provided during other times when not appropriate.

Scribes may be teachers, teacher aides, teacher assistants, or other school personnel who are appropriately trained and qualified. Whenever possible, the student should have the same scribe for state examinations as they have had for classroom tests or other classroom instruction. In all cases, the scribe must understand how to record responses using the procedures described and be familiar with the test, including knowledge of the vocabulary used in the test.

Test Read

When test items are to be read as a result of a testing accommodation, the entire test must be read, including reading passages, questions, multiple choice items, and the rest. Such content may be read more than once in accordance with the individual student's IEP. Students who have difficulty with auditory processing may need content read more than once. To accommodate the individual student's pace, this accommodation is best administered individually rather than in a group setting. The student's IEP would need to note whether an individual or group setting is called for. Content must be read in a neutral manner, without intonation, emphasis, or other means of drawing attention to key words and phrases. Passages and items must be read *word-for-word*, with no clarification, explanation, reordering, or rewording. An exception may be made for tests and quizzes that the teacher has developed and administers. In these instances, test questions and items may be clarified at the discretion of the teacher because the teacher, having developed the assessment, is best able to determine whether, and the extent to which, any clarification may be provided without compromising the test's **validity**. (Any clarification of a question or item on teacher-developed tests is permissible only if it can also be provided to all other students without nullifying the results.) Readers should be trained in how to administer this accommodation in the appropriate manner and should be familiar with the content and vocabulary of the subject being assessed, including the pronunciation of words on the test.

Revised Test Format

If the student's IEP requires a revised test format, the principal is responsible for implementing this accommodation. Changes in test format such as fewer items on a page (a large-print edition has this feature), increased spacing between items, changing size or shape or location of space for answers, and the like can be made by the school.

Revised Test Directions

Revision of test directions is an accommodation that is limited to oral or written instructions provided to all students that explain where and how responses must be recorded; how to proceed in taking the test upon completion of sections; and what steps are required upon completion of the examination. The term *test directions* never refers to any part of a question or passage that appears on a state assessment.

Flexibility in Setting

Setting accommodations can include

- Changes in the *conditions* of the setting, such as special lighting or adaptive furniture
- Changes in the *location itself*, accomplished by moving the student to a separate room

Separate setting means a student is administered the test in a separate room apart from the standard setting being used to administer the test. The student can be administered the test individually or in a small group. The separate setting must be specified on the IEP. In all instances, the special location should be one that is comfortable and appropriate for test administration.

Multiple-Day Administration of State Examinations

Important considerations and procedures associated with this test accommodation are

- Each secondary-level examination must begin on the date scheduled by an office of state assessment (the name of this office may vary in states across the country) for its general administration. At the elementary and intermediate levels, the assessment must begin during the testing period determined by the assessment office on the same day as the general education students' assessment of the same title begins. In the event the student has two tests scheduled on the same day, both tests must begin on that day.

- Students with accommodations indicated on the IEP that permit extended time or to whom the multiple-day accommodation is made available may begin no more than two state assessments on any single day. Students with either of those accommodations who have more than two state assessments scheduled to begin on the same day must postpone one until the next regularly scheduled examination period (January, June, or August) at the earliest.
- The student must receive the amount of extended time indicated on his or her IEP to complete the examination or section(s) administered during a given day.
- Just before beginning a multiple-day administration, the school must separate the examination into clearly defined sections or parts.
- Students may be given individual sections to complete one at a time and may be permitted to start additional sections only if they are expected to complete all those sections on that day. This ensures that there will be no advance knowledge of upcoming sections and content of the test not completed on an earlier day.
- Students who do not complete a section on the day it is begun are not permitted to complete that section on the following day. (Students may be given a photocopy of previous sections they have begun so that they have access to information in these sections, but no changes may be made to student responses provided on any section begun on an earlier day or session.)
- On subsequent testing days, the student will be given additional sections to complete. These sections must be provided one at a time.

Types of Testing Accommodations and Questions to Consider

Flexibility in Setting

- Separate location or room—administer the test individually
- Separate location or room—administer test in a small group (three to five students)
- Provide adaptive or special equipment or furniture (specify type, e.g., study carrel)
- Special lighting (specify type, e.g., 75-watt incandescent light on desk)
- Special acoustics (specify manner, e.g., minimal extraneous noises)

- Location with minimal distraction (specify type, e.g., minimal visual distraction)
- Preferential seating

Examples of Questions to Ask to Determine Whether Setting Accommodations Are Needed

- Do others easily distract the student or does he or she have difficulty remaining on task?
- Does the student require any specialized equipment or other accommodations that may be distracting to others?
- Does the student have visual or auditory impairments that require special lighting or acoustics?
- Can the student focus on his or her own work in a setting with large groups of other students?
- Does the student exhibit behaviors that may disrupt the attention of other students?
- Does the student require any setting accommodations in the classroom?

Flexibility in Scheduling and Timing

- Extended time (specify amount, as in "time and a half")
- Administer tests with frequent breaks (specify duration, e.g., sessions not to exceed 30 minutes with 10-minute breaks)
- Administer state examinations over successive administrations
- Administer state examinations over multiple days

Examples of Questions to Ask to Determine Whether Scheduling Accommodations Are Needed

- Can the student work continuously for the length of time allocated for the standard test administration?
- Does the student use other accommodations or adaptive equipment that require more time for the student to complete test items (e.g., use of scribe, use of head pointer to type)?
- Does the student tire easily because health impairments result in his or her inability to sit for the length of time required to complete the test in one day?
- Does the student's visual impairment decrease his or her working rate or result in eyestrain, requiring frequent breaks?
- Does the student's learning disability affect the rate at which he or she processes written information?

- Does the student's motor disability affect the rate at which he or she writes written responses?
- Does the student take a medication that might require that testing occur during a specific time of day to ensure optimal performance?
- Does the student's attention span or distractibility require shorter working periods and frequent breaks?

Method of Presentation

Revised Test Format
- Braille editions of tests
- Large-type editions of tests
- More spacing between test items
- Larger answer boxes or bubbles
- Fewer test items per page
- Multiple-choice items in vertical format with answer bubble to right of response choices
- Reading passages with one complete sentence per line

Examples of Questions to Ask to Determine
Whether Revised Test Format Accommodations Are Needed
- Are instructional materials used in the classroom provided in a revised format (e.g., nonstandard print or spacing)?
- Does the student have difficulty maintaining his or her place in a standard examination booklet?
- Does the student have a visual, perceptual, or motor impairment that requires large-type or Braille materials?

Revised Test Directions
- Directions read to student
- Directions reread for each page of questions
- Simplified language in directions
- Verbs in directions underlined or highlighted
- Cues (e.g., arrows and stop signs) on answer form
- Additional examples provided

Examples of Questions to Ask to Determine
Whether Revised Test Directions Are Needed
- Is the student able to read and understand directions?
- Is this accommodation provided to the student in the classroom?

- Can the student follow oral directions from an adult or audiotape?
- Does the student need directions repeated frequently?

Revision of test directions is an accommodation that is limited to oral or written instructions provided to all students that explain where and how responses must be recorded, how to proceed in taking the test upon completion of sections, and what steps are required upon completion of the examination. The term *test directions* never refers to any part of a question or passage that appears on a state assessment.

Use of Aids and Assistive Technology
- Audiotape
- Tape recorder
- Computer (including talking word processor)
- Listening section repeated more than the standard number of times
- Listening section signed more than the standard number of times
- Papers secured to work area with tape or magnets
- Test passages, questions, items, and multiple-choice responses read to student
- Test passages, questions, items, and multiple-choice responses signed to student
- Magnification devices (specify type)
- Amplification devices (specify type)

Examples of Questions to Ask to Determine Whether Use of Aids Is Needed
- What aids are used for classroom instruction?
- What assistive technology devices are indicated on the student's IEP?
- Has the student been identified as having a reading disability?
- Does the student have low or poor reading skills that may require the reading of tests or sections of tests that do *not* measure reading comprehension in order for the student to demonstrate knowledge of subject areas?
- Does the student have a hearing impairment and need an interpreter to sign directions or a listening comprehension section?

Method of Response

- Allow marking of answers in the booklet rather than on the answer sheet.
- Allow the use of additional paper for mathematical calculations.

Use of Aids and Assistive Technology
- Amanuensis (scribe)
- Tape recorder
- Word processor
- Communication device
- Pointing to indicate response

Examples of Questions to Ask to Determine Whether Use of Aids Is Needed
- Does the student have difficulty tracking from one paper to another and maintaining his or her place?
- Does the student have a disability that affects the ability to record his or her responses in the standard manner?
- Can the student use a pencil or writing instrument?
- What aids are used in the classroom and for homework assignments (e.g., word processor, adaptive writing instruments, or dictating to a tape recorder or scribe)?

Other

- On-task focusing prompts
- Waiving spelling requirements
- Waiving paragraphing requirements
- Waiving punctuation requirements

Use of Aids and Assistive Technology
- Calculator
- Abacus
- Arithmetic tables
- Spell-check device
- Grammar-check device
- Manipulatives

Examples of Questions to Ask to Determine Whether Use of Aids Is Needed
- Has the student been identified as having a disability that affects his or her ability to spell?
- Has the student been identified as having a disability that affects his or her ability to compute or memorize basic mathematical facts?
- Does the student have a visual or motor disability that affects the ability to use paper and pencil to perform computations?
- Does the student have difficulty staying on task?

Sample

Student Characteristics and Possible Accommodations

Student Characteristics	Possible Effect on Test-Taking	Possible Accommodations
Poor attention or distractibility. Has difficulty remaining on task.	May have difficulty concentrating on test items for extended length of time and completing exam in allotted time. May be distracted by other students.	• Separate setting free from distractions • On-task focusing prompts • Provide breaks during exam period • Extended time
	May have difficulty following or remembering directions.	• Directions read more than standard number of times • Directions provided for each page of questions • Directions simplified
	May have difficulty dividing attention between test booklet and recording answers on a separate answer sheet.	• Record answers directly in test booklet
Processes written information at a slow rate.	May not be able to complete exam within standard timeframe.	• Extended time
	May become fatigued or distracted.	• Separate setting • Directions read orally • Tests read orally
Poor physical and motor coordination; writing difficulties.	Difficulty or unable to record responses using paper and pencil in standard manner.	• Use of computer or word processor or other writing aids • Respond orally to scribe • Separate setting when using scribe • Use of adaptive writing utensils
	Difficulty recording answers on a separate answer sheet.	• Record answers directly in test booklet • Allow additional space for writing
	Writing tasks completed at a slow rate.	• Extended time
	Difficulty or unable to use paper and pencil to solve computations.	• Use of calculator or math tables • Use of graph paper to align numbers when doing computations
Difficulty following or understanding directions.	May not understand what the test requires them to do.	• Directions read orally • Directions simplified • Additional examples of directions provided

Student Characteristics	Possible Effect on Test-Taking	Possible Accommodations
		• Key words or phrases of directions highlighted
	May have difficulty remembering directions.	• Directions reread for each page of questions
Visual impairments	Unable to or has difficulty accessing test in standard print format and requires tactile or oral means to obtain information.	• Braille • Tests read orally • Tape recorder
	May have low or limited vision and has difficulty with standard print.	• Large type • Magnifier • Tests read when fatigue sets in due to eyestrain • Special desk or book stand to hold materials for easier reading • Extended time • Increase spacing between test items • Fewer items per page
	Unable to use paper and pencil to solve computations.	• Use of calculator or talking calculator • Use of graph paper to align numbers
	Difficulty tracking from test to answer sheet.	• Record answers on test booklet • Templates to reduce visible print
	May have low or limited vision and has difficulty with detailed visual tasks such as printed material, graphs, charts, diagrams, etc.	• Highlighting entire graphs to increase contrast from color of page • Special lighting • Oral description of graphs, charts, etc. presented in a neutral manner
	Difficulty maintaining place in a standard test booklet.	• Use of templates to reduce visible print
Visual-perceptual difficulties	Difficulty focusing on individual items if too many items are presented.	• Large type • Increase spacing between test items • Fewer items per page • Use of templates to reduce visible print
Emotional or mental health impairments	Displays test anxiety.	• Extended time • Breaks during test

(Continued)

(Continued)

Student Characteristics	Possible Effect on Test-Taking	Possible Accommodations
	Exhibits inappropriate behavior.	• Separate location • On-task focusing prompts
	Administered medication that may affect the student's physical stamina.	• Test administered during optimal times when student is most alert
Health impairments or poor stamina	Unable to sit for extended lengths of time without changing position.	• Extended time • Breaks provided for rest periods • Adaptive furniture
	Unable to complete test within standard time allotted due to fatigue.	• Multiple-day testing • Separate setting
	Increased fatigue as duration of taking test increases.	• Use of scribe when fatigue affects ability to write • Tests read when fatigue affects ability to read
Difficulty with reading	Reading skills below grade level of test.	• Oral reading of tests or sections of tests that do not measure reading comprehension
	Slow reading pace.	• Test read orally to student individually in a separate location to accommodate individual student pace • Extended time
Hearing impairments	Unable to or has difficulty accessing oral directions or listening sections of test in standard manner.	• Use of sign language interpreter for oral directions and listening passages • Listening passages may be signed more than once • Written directions provided • Extended time • Separate setting • Amplification devices • Preferential seating in front of interpreter
Difficulty with auditory processing	Difficulty remembering or understanding oral directions.	• Repeat directions more than standard number of times • Directions simplified • Provide written directions • Preferential seating • Repeat listening section more than standard number of times
Difficulty with math processing or computations	Unable to memorize basic math facts.	• Use of calculator • Chart of basic math facts

Testing accommodations must be clearly stated to ensure a consistent understanding by the team, school principal, teachers, paraprofessionals, the student, and the student's parents. Specific testing accommodations (e.g., "use of word processor") should be indicated, not generic test accommodation categories (e.g., "answers may be recorded in any manner").

It is appropriate to indicate the conditions or types of tests that will require testing accommodations. Such conditions may include the length of the test, the purpose of the test, the presentation of test items, and the method of response required by the student. As examples: A student with a motor impairment may need a scribe for tests requiring extensive writing such as essay writing, but not for multiple-choice tests; a student may need breaks at certain intervals for tests longer than an hour in length but not for 40-minute classroom tests.

A particular test accommodation may also be needed because of and in conjunction with the provision of another accommodation. For example, separate setting may be needed when the student has the use of a scribe. In such instances, both accommodations must be indicated on the IEP and qualifying conditions would be indicated as appropriate.

If it is determined that the student needs a particular testing accommodation for all tests, then qualifying conditions are not indicated or the IEP would indicate "all tests."

For documenting certain accommodations, the following specifications should be included:

- When documenting extended time, specify the amount of extended time (e.g., time and a half, double time).
- When documenting breaks, specify the duration of the break and at what intervals (e.g., 10-minute break every 40 minutes).
- When documenting separate setting, specify whether as an individual or in a small group.
- When documenting adaptive furniture, special lighting, or acoustics, specify the type (e.g., study carrel).

Qualifying terms requiring case-by-case judgment such as, *as appropriate* or *when necessary,* should not be used on the IEP.

Testing accommodations should not name specific tests (e.g., "calculator with fraction capability," not "calculator with fraction capability on high school exit examination in mathematics").

Sample

Testing Accommodations

The following testing accommodations will be used consistently:

- In the student's education program
- In the administration of districtwide assessments of student achievement
- In the administration of state assessments of student achievement, as consistent with state education department policy

Testing Accommodation	Conditions	Specifications
Extended time	For tests requiring extended writing (essay) responses	Double time
Separate setting	All tests	Small group—quiet with limited visual distractions
Breaks	For tests longer than 40 minutes in length	10-minute break every 40 minutes

Step 10: Determine the Need for Assistive Technology Devices and Services

The IEP must describe any assistive technology devices or services needed for the student to benefit from education, including whether the student requires the use of a school-purchased assistive technology device in the student's home or in other settings in order for the student to receive a free appropriate public education.

- Assistive technology device means any item, piece of equipment, or product system, whether acquired commercially off the shelf, modified, or customized, that is used to increase, maintain, or improve the functional capabilities of a student with a disability. Assistive technology devices can range from low-technology items like pencil grips, markers, or paper stabilizers to high-technology items such as voice synthesizers, Braille readers, or voice-activated computers.
- Assistive technology service means any service that directly assists a student with a disability in the selection, acquisition, or use of an assistive technology device.

When a student needs an assistive technology device or service, the team needs to consider what instruction the student might require to use the assistive technology device as well as any supports and services the student or the student's teachers may need related to the use of the device.

Assistive technology devices and services would be considered supplementary aids and services.

> *Each student's IEP team must consider the student's need for assistive technology (AT) in the development of the student's IEP(300.346(a)(2)(v); and the nature and extent of the AT devices and services to be provided to the student must be reflected in the student's IEP(300.346(c)).*
>
> *A public agency must permit a student to use school-purchased assistive technology devices at home or in other settings, if the IEP team determines that the student needs access to those devices in nonschool settings in order to receive FAPE (to complete homework, for example). Any assistive technology devices that are necessary to ensure FAPE must be provided at no cost to the parents, and the parents cannot be charged for normal use, wear and tear. However, while ownership of the devices in these circumstances would remain with the public agency, State law, rather than Part B, generally would govern whether parents are liable for loss, theft, or damage due to negligence or misuse of publicly owned equipment used at home or in other settings in accordance with a student's IEP. (64 Fed. Reg. [March 12, 1999])*

Assistive technology devices include any item or product system, acquired commercially off the shelf, modified, or customized, that is used to maintain or improve the functional capabilities of a student with a disability. Assistive technology service includes any service that directly assists a student with a disability in the selection, acquisition, or use of an assistive technology device.

The service may include

- The assessment of the needs of a student with a disability, including a functional evaluation of the student in his or her customary environment
- Purchasing, leasing, or otherwise providing assistive technology devices for students with disabilities
- Selecting, designing, customizing, maintaining, repairing, or replacing assistive technology devices
- Coordinating and using other therapies, interventions, or services with assistive technology devices, such as those associated with existing education and rehabilitation plans and programs

- Training or technical assistance for a student with a disability or, if appropriate, that student's family and educators. This training may be ongoing.

An assistive technology service is any service that directly assists an individual with a disability in the selection, acquisition, or use of an assistive technology device. Assistive technology services include

- Evaluation of the technology needs of the individual, including a functional evaluation in the individual's customary environment
- Purchasing, leasing, or otherwise providing for the acquisition of assistive technology devices for individuals with disabilities
- Selecting, designing, fitting, customizing, adapting, applying, retaining, repairing, or replacing of assistive technology devices
- Coordinating and using other therapies, interventions, or services with assistive technology devices, such as those associated with existing education and rehabilitation plans and programs
- Training or technical assistance for an individual with a disability, or, when appropriate, that individual's family
- Training or technical assistance for professionals (including individuals providing education or rehabilitation services), employers, or other individuals who provide services to, employ, or otherwise are substantially involved in the major life functions of individuals with disabilities

Assistive Technology Assessment Process

The assessment process for a student referred for special education may include the consideration of whether assistive technology is necessary for the student to achieve educational goals, benefit from education, or make reasonable progress in the least restrictive educational setting. The evaluation team should be multidisciplinary and may involve occupational therapists, physical therapists, speech-language pathologists, assistive technology specialists, special and general education teachers, adaptive physical education teachers, rehabilitation counselors, parents, and caregivers. At least one member of the team should be knowledgeable in assistive technology.

Assessment of the need for assistive technology devices or assistive technology services is always done in light of the student's ability to access the curriculum. During the assessment process, several means of benefiting from the educational program should be explored and the effectiveness documented.

Assistive Technology Devices and Services Designated in the IEP

If the IEP team determines that the student requires assistive technology in order to access the curriculum and receive FAPE, and the IEP team designates the need for assistive technology as either special education or a related service, the IEP must include a specific statement of such services, including the nature and amount of such services. The inclusion of assistive technology in the IEP requires a degree of specificity so that it is clear how and why the technology will be used to accomplish a particular goal.

Assistive technology can be a form of supplementary aid or service utilized to facilitate a student's education in a general educational environment. Such supplementary aids and services, or modifications to the general education program, must be included in a student's IEP. Individually prescribed devices such as glasses or hearing aids are generally considered to be personal items and are not a service to be provided by the district and thus would not be listed as a service need on the IEP.

Technology devices and services designated in the IEP must be provided at no cost to the parents. However, the district does not need to provide assistive devices if a meaningful and beneficial education can be provided to the student without the equipment.

Ownership of Equipment

Technology devices purchased by the school district belong to the district. Distribution and use of devices are under the district's control as long as the needs designated in the IEP are being met. School district insurance policies usually cover devices purchased by the district for use by a student. Devices purchased with other funding sources may or may not be insured while on school premises. School staff and parents may want to investigate the district's property insurance to determine what is currently covered and whether the policy insures against loss or damage of assistive devices.

In general, the district is responsible for repair and maintenance of assistive devices used to support programs described in the IEP.

The use of school-purchased assistive technology devices in a student's home or in other settings is required if the student's IEP team determines that this particular student needs access to those particular devices in order to receive FAPE.

Sample

Assistive Technology Devices and Services

Assistive Technology Devices and Services	Frequency	Duration	Location	Initiation Date
Computer program graphic organizer	Daily	Writing Assignments	English class History class	10/14/02

Step 11: Determine the Supports for School Personnel on Behalf of the Student

Supports for school personnel are those that would help them to more effectively work with the student. This could include, for example, special training for a student's teacher to meet a unique and specific need of the student. The IEP must describe the supports for school personnel that will be provided on behalf of the student in order for the student to advance toward attaining the annual goals, to be involved in and progress in the general curriculum, and to participate in extracurricular and other nonacademic activities. These supports for school personnel are those that are needed to meet the unique and specific needs of the student.

Examples of supports that may be provided for school personnel are

- Information on a specific disability and implications for instruction
- Training in use of specific positive behavioral interventions
- Training in the use of American Sign Language
- Assistance with curriculum modifications
- Behavioral consultation with a school psychologist, social worker, or other behavioral consultant

Sample

Supports for School Personnel on Behalf of Student

Supports for School Personnel on Behalf of Student	Frequency	Duration	Location	Initiation Date
Consult with behavior management counselor	1 time per month for 3 months	30 minutes	Staff meeting room	10/14/02

Step 12: Determine the Ability of a Student to Participate in State and District Assessments

Consistent with Sec. 300.138 (a), which sets forth a presumption that students with disabilities will be included in general statewide and districtwide assessment programs, and provided with appropriate accommodations if necessary, Sec. 300.347 (a) (5) requires that the IEP for each student with a disability include "*(i) a statement of any individual modifications in the administration of State or districtwide assessments of student achievement that are needed in order for the student to participate in the assessment; and (ii) if the IEP team determines that the student will not participate in a particular State or districtwide assessment of student achievement (or part of an assessment of student achievement), a statement of—(A) Why that assessment is not appropriate for the student; and (B) How the student will be assessed.*"

To meet the requirements in this component, the IEP team reviews present levels of educational performance and annual goals to decide what the student should know and be able to do before determining the assessment needs of the student. Then the IEP team reviews and discusses the statement of special education, related services, and supplementary services and aids to be provided to the student.

The IEP team determines the provisions that must be made to allow the student to access and demonstrate learning by considering the following:

- Classroom organization and management
- Setting
- Assignments
- Scheduling
- Presentation
- Response
- Timing
- Technology

When considering the setting, the IEP team discusses issues to

- Determine whether the student is able to focus on his or her work with 25 or 30 other students in a setting
- Determine whether the student displays behaviors that are distracting to others

- Ascertain whether the student can listen to and follow oral directions given by an adult or take a test in the same way as it is administered to other students. If the student is unable to focus in a large group, or displays behaviors that are distracting to others, then the student may need accommodations both in instruction and assessment, such as small group, study carrel, or minimally distracting environment.

To determine the substantial changes in what the student is expected to learn and demonstrate, consider these:

- Changing the instructional (grade) level
- Decreasing the number of concepts to be mastered
- Modifying the content standards or performance objectives in the standards
- Changing performance criteria

To determine what modifications to provide, the team must consider the student's instructional levels and organizational grade level in the present levels of performance. If the student is in the sixth grade, but reading and writing skills are at a third-grade level and the mathematics level is fourth grade, then the IEP team will need to consider modifying the grade levels. If the goals in the content standards have been adapted (divided into smaller parts) and the performance objectives have been modified, the IEP team will need to determine what modifications in instruction and assessment will be consistent with those changes.

If the IEP team makes the determination that the student will *not* participate in the state or district assessment or some part of such an assessment, a statement of why that assessment is not appropriate, including an explanation of how the student will be assessed, must be stated clearly in the IEP. The IEP team discusses and determines the resulting assessment programs, modifications, and accommodations. The IEP team members must understand that the accommodations and the modifications in instruction and assessment must be aligned to the extent appropriate.

The IEP team

- Considers the accommodations and modifications being made in instruction
- Develops additional accommodations and modifications for each student based on his or her individual strengths

- Identifies the level of assessment to be administered, having based it on the level within the standard that is being addressed and its content area
- Determines the need for additional accommodations and modifications in the administration of the assessments selected
- Documents instructional and assessment modifications and accommodations in the IEP

Sample

Participation in Assessments

[X] Student will participate in the same state or local assessments that are administered to general education students.

[ ] The following state or local assessments (or part of an assessment) that are administered to general education students are not appropriate for the student:

Assessment(s): _____

Reason not appropriate: _____

How student will be assessed:

[ ] Alternate assessment for students with severe disabilities

[ ] Other: _____

Step 13: Determine Extended School Year (ESY) Services

The Law

According to 20 U.S.C. § 1414 (d) (1) (A) (v),

(a) (1) Each public agency shall ensure that extended school year services are available as necessary to provide FAPE, consistent with this paragraph (a) (2) of this section. (2) Extended school year services must be provided only if a student's IEP team determines, on an individual basis, in accordance with §§300.340–300.350, that the services are necessary for the provision of FAPE to the student. In implementing this requirement in this section, a public agency may not— (I) Limit extended school year services to particular categories of disability; or (ii) Unilaterally limit the type, amount, or duration of those services.

Definition

Extended school year services means special education and related services that meet state standards and are provided to a student with a disability

- Beyond the normal school year
- In accordance with the student's IEP
- At no cost to the parents of the student

Purpose

The goal of an ESY program is to assist students with disabilities with the emergence, maintenance, or critical generalization of specific IEP objectives learned the year preceding the ESY. These may include goals related to self-sufficiency, behavior, socialization, communication, and academics. ESY services for students receiving special education provide a focus different from that of general summer school programs.

Determination of the Need for ESY

Students qualify for ESY services in three general areas:

- Emerging skill
- Regression or recoupment
- Self-sufficiency

ESY services must be provided only if a student's IEP team determines, for this individual case, that the services are necessary for the provision of FAPE to the student. Provision of ESY services for one year does not mean that the student needs such services each year. A district may not limit ESY services to particular disability categories or unilaterally limit the type, amount, or duration of those services.

ESY services can be based on one or more of three general areas according to the following guidelines. A "yes" response to all questions within one area provides a strong indication that ESY services are warranted.

Emerging Skill

When few, if any, gains are made during the regular school year and a critical skill is in the process of emerging, and it is believed that with ESY services the student could make reasonable gains, then ESY services must be considered. Collect documentation to assist the IEP team in determining the following:

- Does progress toward the goals and objectives or benchmarks over an extended period show few, if any, gains?
- Is a skill emerging?
- Does documentation support that ESY services are needed to avoid irreparable loss of the learning opportunity?

Regression or Recoupment

When the student would regress to such an extent and the amount of time required to relearn skills or behaviors becomes so significant that he or she would be unable to benefit from his or her special education program, then ESY services must be considered. Collect documentation to assist the IEP team in determining the following:

- Do progress reports and data show that the student demonstrates periodic regression that is related to breaks in instruction throughout the school year?
- Do progress reports and data show that the student regresses and cannot relearn the skills in a reasonable amount of time after the breaks?
- Does documentation support that without ESY services the student would regress to such an extent and have such limited recoupment ability that he or she would be unable to benefit from his or her special education program?

Self-Sufficiency

When an interruption in services would threaten the acquisition of critical life skills that aid in the student's ability to function as independently as possible, and those life skills would reduce the student's reliance on caretakers or other institutionalized care, ESY services must be considered. The IEP team should collect documentation to assist in determining the following:

- Does documentation identify critical life skills that are needed for independence?
- Will failure to maintain acquired critical life skills cause major or permanent loss of the skills and create a dependence on caregivers?
- Without ESY services, would the student fail to maintain these critical life skills?

ESY IEP Development

ESY services must be clearly delineated in an IEP. The district can meet this requirement by amending the current IEP on an amendment form or developing a complete ESY IEP. Both require an IEP team meeting and prior written notice to parents. The district must ensure that personnel responsible for implementing the ESY IEP have access to the IEP.

- To be considered for ESY services, the student must be identified as having a disability and must currently be receiving special education services and related services as defined by an IEP.
- Determination of the need for ESY must be made only for the immediate period of interruption of the instructional program. The provision of ESY for the immediate period does not imply that ESY will be required for subsequent periods.
- The critical skills that are the focus of the ESY services are best determined at the time of the development of the annual IEP. An IEP meeting may, however, be convened during the year to review the need for ESY. The ESY program developed should reflect the current goals and objectives or benchmarks from the IEP. It must also consider the student's ability to acquire the skill and be a priority for the student's developmental age.
- The student's educational program is based on individual needs and is not determined by what programs are readily available within the district.
- The student cannot be required to fail, or to go for an entire year without ESY services, simply to prove that a need exists.
- The IEP team shall determine the duration, frequency, and type of services that each student shall receive during the ESY. The goals and objectives or benchmarks should be continuations of all or part of the previous year's IEP, although ESY instruction may be modified in order to enhance emergence, maintenance, or generalization of a skill.
- School districts shall not automatically or categorically exclude or include any student or group from consideration for ESY services.
- ESY services may include special education or related services.
- While ESY services must be provided in the least restrictive environment, districts are not required to create new programs as a means of providing ESY services to students with disabilities in integrated settings if the district does not provide services at that time for its students without disabilities.

- Districts may provide ESY services in a noneducational setting if the IEP team determines it is appropriate.
- ESY services must be provided when ordered by a due process hearing officer. If the district chooses to appeal, the student must be provided with ESY services pending the result of the appeals process.

In Case of a Dispute

It is important for the district to make decisions on the provision of ESY for a student early enough in the school year to allow parents time to exhaust administrative remedies if they disagree with the decision of the IEP team. In the event that a parent disagrees with the decision of the team not to provide ESY services, and the district has not allowed sufficient time for the parents to dispute the decision through due process, the student must be provided with ESY services pending the outcome of the administrative proceedings.

Parents should be given a reasonable amount of time after being notified to respond to a district's decision to not provide ESY services to their child. If a timely response is not received from the parents, then the district is not required to provide the student with ESY services pending the outcome of administrative proceedings. Any time restrictions should be reasonable and be clearly explained or otherwise made known to the parents.

There is no single criterion used in making an eligibility determination for ESY services. One standard is the regression or recoupment analysis. The IEP team would determine whether the degree of regression the student is experiencing jeopardizes his or her ability to learn during the regular school year, and the amount of time needed for the student to regain the skills learned, leading to the overall ability to make meaningful progress.

Other factors to consider:

- The nature and severity of the student's disability
- The ability of the student's parents to provide educational structure at home
- The student's behavioral and physical needs
- Emerging skills and breakthrough opportunities
- The ability of the student to interact with nondisabled peers
- The student's vocational needs
- Areas of the student's curriculum that need attention

Consideration of a broad range of detailed information such as parent and teacher communications, work samples, test results, homework, report cards, progress reports, and parent observations are all helpful in determining the student's ability to reach and maintain his or her identified goals and objectives. Creating a schedule for collecting this information allows the IEP team to review a student's progress toward his or her IEP goals and objectives to better determine the student's need for special education services during school breaks.

Steps for Determining ESY

The IEP team reviews and considers

- The current IEP or individualized family service plan (IFSP; present levels of educational performance, annual goals, objectives, etc.)
- Progress reports of annual goals
- Regression and recoupment evidence
- Information provided by parents and teachers or early interventionists
- Critical learning stages
- Classroom data and observations
- Other data and procedures consistent with district or charter school procedures for determining eligibility for ESY services

Then the IEP team determines

- Whether the student experienced regression and its level of significance
- Whether the student recouped losses within an acceptable time period
- Whether goals of self-sufficiency and independence are being met
- Whether skills or behavior are emerging that are unique to a critical learning period
- The student's eligibility for ESY services
- Skills and behaviors to be included in ESY services to prevent irreparable harm to the student

At this time, the IEP team documents

- Eligibility for ESY
- Annual goals, benchmarks, or short-term objectives to be targeted

- Services, adaptations, and supports needed for ESY
- Initiation date, frequency and amount, duration, and location of services, accommodations and modification, and supports for ESY

If the IEP team determines that insufficient data exist to make a determination on ESY services for the student, a statement of why that determination cannot be made and when eligibility will be reconsidered should be entered.

Step 14: A Statement of Secondary Transition Service Needs and Needed Transition Services for Students

It is crucial for IEP teams to begin planning for a student's lifelong outcomes while the student is still in school. A statement of the transition service needs of the student under the applicable components of the IEP that focus on the student's course of study (such as participation in drivers' education courses, a vocational education program, or general education curriculum) must be included in the IEP by the student's 16th birthday, or earlier if it is determined to be appropriate by the IEP team.

A statement of transition services including courses of study needed to assist the student in reaching postsecondary goals must be in the IEP. Appropriate measurable goals should be based on age-appropriate transition assessments related to training, education, employment, and where appropriate, independent living skills (20 U.S.C. § 1414 (d) (1) (A) (i) (VIII)).

Transition planning and transition services are based on the individual student's needs, taking into account the student's preferences and interests, and must include (1) instruction, (2) related services, (3) community experiences, (4) the development of employment and other adult living objectives, and, when appropriate, (5) acquisition of daily living skills, and (6) functional vocational evaluation.

The transition statement must also include, when appropriate, a statement of the interagency responsibilities or linkages before the student leaves the school setting. If a participating agency other than the educational agency fails to provide agreed-upon services contained in the IEP, the district must reconvene the IEP team to identify alternative strategies for meeting the transition objectives outlined in the student's IEP.

The IEP for each student, beginning not later than the IEP in effect when the student turns 16 (or younger if determined appropriate by the IEP team), must include a statement of appropriate measurable postsecondary goals based upon age-appropriate transition assessments related to training, education, employment, and, where appropriate, independent living skills and the transition services (one of which might be the student's courses of study needed to assist the student in reaching those goals). The statement of transition service needs identifies and plans for educational courses (required, elective, modified, or specially designed courses as well as other educational experiences in the school or the community) that the student will be taking in each grade after becoming 16 years old.

The IEP team must also consider, at a minimum, the following areas: instruction, related services, community experiences, employment, and adult living objectives. If the team determines it to be appropriate, then the statement must also address daily living skills and the need for a functional vocational evaluation. While the IEP team may determine that a student does not require services in all transition planning areas, the decision should be based on the individual needs of the student after carefully considering each planning area. A brief description of each planning area follows:

- *Instruction:* Use of formal techniques to impart knowledge; typically provided in schools but could be provided by other entities in other locations
- *Related services:* Transportation and such developmental, corrective, and other supportive services as are required to assist a student with a disability to benefit from special education
- *Community experiences:* Services provided outside the school building, in community settings or other agencies
- *Employment or other adult living objectives:* Services that lead to a job or career and important adult activities; services could be provided by schools or other agencies
- *Daily living skills (when appropriate):* Activities adults do every day; services could be provided by schools or other agencies
- *Functional vocational evaluation (when appropriate):* Assessment that provides information about job or career interest, aptitudes, and skills; assessments could be provided by school or other agencies

Definition

Transition services means a coordinated set of activities for a student with a disability, designed within an outcome-oriented process, that promotes movement from school to lifetime activities. Lifetime activities include

- Postsecondary education
- Vocational training
- Integrated competitive employment (including supported employment)
- Continuing and adult education
- Adult services
- Independent living or community participation

Transition services should be those that assist the student to reach his or her projected adulthood outcomes.

Law

(34) TRANSITION SERVICES—The term "transition services" means a coordinated set of activities for a student with a disability that—

(A) is designed to be within a results-oriented process, that is focused on improving the academic and functional achievement of the student with a disability to facilitate the student's movement from school to post-school activities, including post-secondary education, vocational education, integrated employment (including supported employment), continuing and adult education, adult services, independent living, or community participation;

(B) is based on the individual student's needs, taking into account the student's strengths, preferences, and interests; and

(C) includes instruction, related services, community experiences, the development of employment and other post-school adult living objectives, and, when appropriate, acquisition of daily living skills and functional vocational evaluation.

(aa) appropriate measurable postsecondary goals based upon age appropriate transition assessments related to training, education, employment, and, where appropriate, independent living skills;

(bb) the transition services (including courses of study) needed to assist the student in reaching those goals;

Requirements

When the student is 14 years old and every year thereafter, the IEP must begin to include a statement of the transition service needs of the student that focus on the student's courses of study (such as participation in advanced placement courses or a vocational education program).

When the student is 15 years old (or younger, if appropriate), the IEP must begin to include a statement of the needed transition services and include a statement of the responsibilities of the school district and, when applicable, participating agencies for the provision of services and activities that promote movement from school to adulthood opportunities, or both, before the student leaves the school setting. The IEP must include those transition services and activities in each of the following areas as appropriate to the needs of the individual student:

- Instruction
- Related services
- Employment and other adult living objectives
- Community living experiences
- Activities of daily living, if appropriate
- Functional vocational assessment, if appropriate

Purpose of Transition Planning and Transition Programs and Services

Transition planning focuses attention on how the student's educational program can be planned to help the student make a successful transition to his or her goals for life after high school, including

- Providing instruction and courses of study that are meaningful to the student's future and will motivate the student to complete his or her education
- Teaching students the skills and knowledge needed in adult life (including career development and occupational skills)
- Providing contacts (linkages) with adult agencies to provide a smooth transition

Statement of Needed Transition Services

The statements of needed transition services, developed in consideration of the student's needs, preferences, and interests, should specify the particular activity or service and the participating agency (that is, the school district or another agency) providing the service. The beginning date for the service should be provided if the date of initiation is different from the date that the IEP is initiated.

Instruction

The IEP must identify any instruction or specific courses that the student might need to prepare the student for adult living. Instruction could include specific general and special education course instruction, career and technical education, or advanced placement courses and instruction to learn a particular skill (e.g., instruction in problem-solving skills, how to use public transportation, how to use a particular assistive technology device, how to balance a checkbook).

Related Services

The IEP must identify any related services (e.g., rehabilitation counseling services, job coach, school social work, orientation and mobility services) the student may need as a transition service to support him or her in attaining the projected adulthood outcomes. (Related services recommended as a transition activity must also be documented under the IEP section "Special Education Program and Services.")

Employment and Other Adult Living Objectives

The IEP must identify what services or activities the student needs in order to prepare him or her for employment and to assist the student in meeting other adult living objectives (e.g., participation in a work experience program, assistance with completing college or employment applications, practice in interviewing skills, travel training).

Community Experiences

The IEP must indicate if a student needs to participate in community-based experiences or learn to access community resources (e.g., afterschool jobs, use of the public library, community recreational activities) to achieve his or her projected adulthood outcomes.

Activities of Daily Living

If appropriate to the needs of the student, the IEP must indicate the services or activities that will assist the student in activities of daily living skills (e.g., dressing, hygiene, self-care skills, and self-medication).

Functional Vocational Assessment

The IEP must indicate if the student will need a functional vocational assessment as a transition service or activity. A functional vocational assessment is an assessment to determine a student's strengths, abilities, and needs in an actual or simulated work setting or in real or simulated work experiences.

Definition of a Participating Agency

Participating agency means a state or local agency, other than the public agency responsible for a student's education, that is financially and legally responsible for providing transition services to the student.

When an agency agrees to provide a service, the IEP must include the service and the implementation date of the service if it is different from the date that the IEP is implemented.

What if the Participating Agency Fails to Provide Services as Planned?

If a participating agency fails to provide agreed-upon transition services contained in the student's IEP, the district responsible for the student's education must, as soon as possible, initiate a meeting to identify alternative strategies to meet the transition objectives, and if necessary, revise the student's IEP.

The Recommended Coordinated Set of Transition Activities

- Are based on individual needs and correspond to careers and real life skills
- Are based on assessment information, including vocational assessment
- Promote movement from school to adult employment, education, and community living
- Focus on the student's strengths, interests, and abilities
- Assist the student to realize the projected adulthood outcomes
- Address instruction and courses of study from the age of 14
- Address instruction, related services, community experiences, and preparation for employment and other adult living objectives, and, when appropriate, acquisition of daily living skills and functional vocational evaluation from the age of 15

- Reflect involvement and connections with general and career and technical education programs as well as supports and programs available after the end of schooling
- Are developed with students and parents as active participants
- Clearly identify the responsibilities of the school district and other agencies

Procedures

To meet the requirements in this component, the IEP team focuses attention on how the student's educational program can be planned to help the student make a successful transition to his or her goals for life after secondary school. It is important that the statement of transition service needs relate directly to the student's goals beyond secondary education and show how planned studies are linked to these goals.

For example, a student interested in exploring a career in computer science may have a statement of transition services needs connected to technology course work while another student's statement of transition services needs could describe why public bus transportation training is important for future independence in the community. Although the focus of transition planning process may shift as the student approaches graduation, the IEP team must begin to discuss specific areas when the student reaches the age of 14 years and must review these areas annually.

When the student is 14 years old or younger, the IEP team, in determining appropriate measurable goals, benchmarks, and services for a student, must begin to determine what instruction and educational experiences will assist the student to prepare for needed transition services. The purpose of the transition service needs is to focus on the planning of a student's course of study during the secondary experiences.

The student's course of study may include

- Elective courses
- Modified instructional opportunities
- Specially selected classes and instruction (such as participation in advanced-placement courses or a vocational education program)
- Any other educational experiences that differ from the course requirements for all other students

These classes and instructional opportunities should be designed to be meaningful to the student's future and motivate the student to complete his education by

- Graduation with a regular diploma
- Completion of a secondary program
- Achievement of the student's desired adulthood goals

When the student reaches the age of 16, and younger if appropriate, the IEP team must begin to focus attention on how the student's educational program can be planned to help the student make a successful transition to his or her goals for life after secondary school. For example, if the student's transition goal is a job, a transition service could be teaching the student how to get to the jobsite on public transportation. The coordinated set of activities must be based on the individual student's needs, taking into account the student preferences and interests, and includes

- Instruction
- Related services
- Community experiences
- The development of employment objectives
- The development of other adult living objectives
- The acquisition of daily living skills, if appropriate
- A functional vocational evaluation, if appropriate

For each specified area, the IEP team must either

- Develop and identify goals to address the identified area, or
- Describe a plan for providing services in that area

Also from the time the student is 16, the IEP team should begin to consider what interagency responsibilities or linkages might be needed. Indicate which agencies will

- Provide or pay for services while the student is still in school
- Provide services to the student after leaving school
- Need to be contacted to determine the eligibility of the student for services before he or she leaves school

If the participating agency fails to provide the transition services described in the IEP, the public agency will convene the IEP team to identify alternative strategies to meet the transition objectives for the student set out in the IEP.

Sample

Coordinated Set of Transition Activities (School to Adulthood)

- For students ages 14 and older, courses of study (that is, instructional activities and educational experiences) to meet transition needs
- For students from the age of 15 (and younger if deemed appropriate), needed transition services and activities in each area

Coordinated Set of Transition Activities	Activity	School District or Agency Responsible	Date
Instruction	Resource room to address organization strategies	Home district	10/14/02
	Horticulture class	ABC Career and Technical Education Center	1/4/03
Related Services	Counseling services	Home district	10/14/02
	Job coach	Youth Career Support Services, Inc	1/3/03
Development of Employment or Other Postschool Adult Living Objectives	Resume development; interview skills; application completion	Youth Career Support Services, Inc.	3/1/03
Community Experience	3 community experiences with job coaching— florist; retail; landscaping	Youth Career Support Services, Inc.	1/3/03
Acquisition of Daily Living Skills	NA		
Functional Vocational Assessment	Situational assessment with job experiences	Youth Career Support Services, Inc.	1/3/03

Step 15: Develop a Statement of Transfer of Parental Rights to the Student Upon Reaching the Age of Majority

Law

> *(cc) Beginning not later than 1 year before the student reaches the age of majority under State law, a statement that the student has been informed of the student's rights under this title, if any, that will transfer to the student on reaching the age of majority under section 615(m).*

The IEP must include a statement that the student has been informed of his or her rights under IDEA 2004 that will transfer to the student on reaching the age of majority (age 18) beginning at least one year before the student reaches the age of majority.

Procedures

To meet the requirement in this component, the IEP team discusses the rights under the IDEA to be transferred to the student at least one year before he or she reaches the age of majority.

The IEP team

- Discusses the rights to be transferred
- Reviews the records and legal documents, as necessary
- Provides notice to the parent(s) and student of the transfer of rights
- Records the date that the student and parents were informed of the rights transferred
- Maintains a copy of the notification sent to the student and parents
- Sends future notices to both the student and the parents

Annual Review and Revision of the IEP

Each student with a disability must have his or her IEP reviewed at least annually. It can be reviewed sooner if a parent or teacher feels that the program and services defined on the student's IEP are not meeting the student's needs. The participants at the meeting should review the student's current IEP to determine whether the goals and objectives have been met (that is, whether the criteria specified for the individual objectives have been achieved).

In order to make this determination, each service provider should have gathered specific information through observation, teacher-made or commercial tests, work samples, and other relevant material. If the goals and objectives have not been met, the service provider should be able to offer specific reasons based on the information she or he has gathered.

Parents, teachers, or others can request that an IEP meeting be held for purposes of review or revision. The decision on if, when, and where the meeting will be held rests with the district, although collaboration with parents is expected. The district should grant any reasonable request for an IEP meeting from any participant. Any changes in an IEP, including changes in the short-term objectives or benchmarks, and changes in the amount of services listed in the IEP, require an IEP meeting.

> *To the extent possible, the local educational agency shall encourage the consolidation of reevaluation meetings for the student and other IEP team meetings for the student (20 U.S.C. § 1414 (d) (3) (E)).*
>
> *A public agency must initiate and conduct meetings periodically, but at least once every twelve months, to review each student's IEP, in order to determine whether the annual goals for the student are being achieved, and to revise the IEP, as appropriate, to address: (a) Any lack of expected progress toward the annual goals and in the general curriculum, if appropriate; (b) the results of any reevaluation; (c) information about the student provided to, or by, the parents; (d) the student's anticipated needs; or (e) other matters.*
>
> *A public agency also must ensure that an IEP is in effect for each student at the beginning of each school year. . . . It must ensure that the IEP contains the necessary special education and related services and supplementary aids and services to ensure that the student's IEP can be appropriately implemented during the next school year.*
>
> *Otherwise, it would be necessary for the public agency to conduct another IEP meeting. Although the public agency is responsible for determining when it is necessary to conduct an IEP meeting, the parents of a student with a disability have the right to request an IEP meeting at any time. For example, if the parents believe that the student is not progressing satisfactorily or that there is a problem with the student's current IEP, it would be appropriate for the parents to request an IEP meeting.*

(Continued)

(Continued)

> *If a student's teacher feels that the student's IEP or placement is not appropriate for the student, the teacher should follow agency procedures with respect to: (1) calling or meeting with the parents or (2) requesting the agency to hold another IEP meeting to review the student's IEP.*
>
> The legislative history of Public Law 94-142 makes it clear that there should be as many meetings a year as any one student may need (121 Cong. Rec. S20428-29 (Nov. 19, 1975) (remarks of Senator Stafford)). Public agencies should grant any reasonable parent request for an IEP meeting. For example, if the parents question the adequacy of services that are provided while their child is suspended for short periods of time, it would be appropriate to convene an IEP meeting (64 Fed. Reg. 12,476–12,477 [March 12, 1999]).

Who Must Participate in the Meeting to Review the IEP?

The IEP team needs to conduct the review of the IEP. Team members include

- The student's parents
- At least one general education teacher of the student
- At least one special education teacher of the student
- A representative of the LEA
- An individual who can interpret the implications of evaluation results
- Other individuals who have knowledge of or special expertise with the student (at the discretion of the parent or agency). This includes related service providers as appropriate.
- The student when it is deemed appropriate

If the student is 14 years of age, or younger if appropriate, transition services participants need to attend the meeting.

Who Can Initiate the IEP Review or Revision Meetings, and When Shall They Take Place?

The regulations state that a student's IEP must be in effect at the beginning of each school year. Meetings must be conducted periodically, but not less than once every twelve months. These meetings are initiated and conducted at the discretion of the public agency.

Professionals who work with the student and parents may determine that an IEP meeting is warranted to provide FAPE to the student at any time during the twelve months.

Purpose of an IEP Review

The IEP review is conducted to accomplish the following purposes:

- To determine whether the student's annual goals are being achieved
- To revise the IEP if there is any lack of expected progress toward annual goals and in the general education curriculum, when appropriate
- To determine whether an additional assessment is necessary and address the results of those conducted
- To address information about the student provided to, or by, the parents
- To monitor the continuing eligibility of the student
- To write a new IEP with revised goals and objectives to meet the student's anticipated needs for the next year

IEP Changes at Times Other Than the Annual Review

When changes in the IEP are required at times other than the annual review date, these changes may be discussed and implemented through a scheduled IEP meeting utilizing one of the following options:

- Review the entire plan and establish a new annual review date.
- Use an amendment form. When this option is used, the change becomes a part of the IEP and must be reviewed on the IEP's original annual review date.
- Changes on the current IEP can be made by agreement between the parent and the district (20 U.S.C. § 1414 (d) (3) (F)).

In making changes to a student's IEP after the annual IEP meeting for a school year, the parent of a student with a disability and the local educational agency may agree not to convene an IEP meeting for the purposes of making such changes, and instead may develop a written document to amend or modify the student's current IEP (20 U.S.C. § 1414 (d) (3) (D)).

Amendments to the IEP can be made either by the entire IEP team (or the parent and the LEA may agree not to convene an IEP meeting) by amending the IEP rather than redrafting the entire IEP. Upon request, a parent shall be provided with a revised copy of the IEP with the amendments incorporated (20 U.S.C. § 1414 (d) (3) (F)).

Recommendations Upon Declassification

A school district must evaluate a student with a disability prior to determining that the student is no longer a student with a disability. A student with a disability who has been reevaluated and determined by the team to no longer be eligible for special education services should have declassification recommendations documented on his or her final IEP.

The team should determine what IEP recommendations will continue upon the student's declassification, including, as appropriate

- Testing accommodations
- The student's continued exemption from the Language Other Than English Requirement

The team must also identify needed declassification support services to be provided to the student and the student's teachers during the first year after the student is declassified.

Testing Accommodations

Upon declassification, the committee on special education (CSE; sometimes referred to as the eligibility committee) may determine that the effects of a student's disability may continue to prevent the student from demonstrating the achievement of certain knowledge and skills and, as a result, the student may continue to need the testing accommodations previously documented on the IEP. If such a determination is made, the testing accommodations must be documented in the recommendation for declassification.

Continued Exemption From Language Other Than English Requirement

If, prior to declassification, the CSE has determined that a student has a disability that adversely affects the ability to learn a language and has excused the student from the Language Other Than English Requirement for graduation, and this has been documented on the IEP, this exemption would continue upon declassification. It is recommended that this continued exemption be documented on the student's last IEP.

Declassification Support Services

Declassification support services means services provided to a student or a student's teacher in the first year that a student moves from a special education program to a full-time general education program to aid the student in moving from special education to full-time general education, including

- *For the student,* psychological services, social work services, speech and language improvement services, noncareer counseling, and other appropriate general education support services
- *For the student's teacher,* the assistance of a teacher aide or a teaching assistant and consultation with appropriate personnel

Recommendations for declassification support services must include

- The projected date of initiation of such services
- The frequency of provision of services
- The duration of such services (provided that such services for state aid purposes may be provided for up to one year after the student enters the full-time general education program)

Implementation of
Recommendations Upon Declassification

Upon a recommendation of declassification, the team is responsible to ensure that the declassification recommendations are implemented. This means that

- A copy of the student's last IEP, with the declassification recommendations, must be provided to the student's general education teachers and providers
- The team chairperson must designate an individual knowledgeable about the student's program to inform the student's teachers and others (e.g., school principal or guidance counselor) of their specific responsibilities to implement the declassification recommendations on the student's last IEP

Sample

Recommendations Upon Declassification

Date Declassified: 10/1/05

IEP recommendations to continue upon declassification:

Testing Accommodations	Conditions	Specifications
Extended time	For tests requiring extended writing (essay) responses	Double time
Separate setting	All tests	Small group
Breaks	For tests longer than 40 minutes in length	10-minute break every 40 minutes

Continued Eligibility for Local Diploma ("Safety Net"): Yes [X] No [ ]
Continued "Language Other Than English" Exemption: Yes [X] No [ ]

Declassification Support Services to be provided during the first year that a student moves from a special education program to a full-time general education program.

Service	Initiation Date	Frequency	Duration	Ending Date
Psychological services	10/1/05	1 time per month	1 hour	6/30/06

Appendix

Individuals with Disabilities Education Improvement Act of 2004—Section on IEPs (Enrolled as Agreed to or Passed by Both House and Senate)

(d) INDIVIDUALIZED EDUCATION PROGRAMS—

(1) DEFINITIONS—In this title:

(A) INDIVIDUALIZED EDUCATION PROGRAM—

(i) IN GENERAL—The term "individualized education program" or "IEP" means a written statement for each student with a disability that is developed, reviewed, and revised in accordance with this section and that includes—

(I) a statement of the student's present levels of academic achievement and functional performance, including—

(aa) how the student's disability affects the student's involvement and progress in the general education curriculum;

(bb) for preschool students, as appropriate, how the disability affects the student's participation in appropriate activities; and (cc) for students with disabilities who take alternate assessments aligned to alternate achievement standards, a description of benchmarks or short-term objectives;

(II) a statement of measurable annual goals, including academic and functional goals, designed to—

(aa) meet the student's needs that result from the student's disability to enable the student to be involved in and make progress in the general education curriculum; and

(bb) meet each of the student's other educational needs that result from the student's disability;

(III) a description of how the student's progress toward meeting the annual goals described in subclause (II) will be measured and when periodic reports on the progress the student is making toward meeting the annual goals (such as through the use of quarterly or other periodic reports, concurrent with the issuance of report cards) will be provided;

(IV) a statement of the special education and related services and supplementary aids and services, based on peer-reviewed research to the extent practicable, to be provided to the student, or on behalf of the student, and a statement of the program modifications or supports for school personnel that will be provided for the student—

(aa) to advance appropriately toward attaining the annual goals;

(bb) to be involved in and make progress in the general education curriculum in accordance with subclause (I) and to participate in extracurricular and other nonacademic activities; and

(cc) to be educated and participate with other students with disabilities and nondisabled students in the activities described in this subparagraph;

(V) an explanation of the extent, if any, to which the student will not participate with nondisabled students in the regular class and in the activities described in subclause (IV)(cc);

(VI)

(aa) a statement of any individual appropriate accommodations that are necessary to measure the academic achievement and functional performance of the student on State and districtwide assessments consistent with section 612(a)(16)(A); and

(bb) if the IEP Team determines that the student shall take an alternate assessment on a particular State or districtwide assessment of student achievement, a statement of why—

(AA) the student cannot participate in the regular assessment; and

(BB) the particular alternate assessment selected is appropriate for the student;

(VII) the projected date for the beginning of the services and modifications described in subclause (IV), and the anticipated frequency, location, and duration of those services and modifications; and

(VIII) beginning not later than the first IEP to be in effect when the student is 16, and updated annually thereafter—

(aa) appropriate measurable postsecondary goals based upon age appropriate transition assessments related to training, education, employment, and, where appropriate, independent living skills;

(bb) the transition services (including courses of study) needed to assist the student in reaching those goals; and

(cc) beginning not later than 1 year before the student reaches the age of majority under State law, a statement that the student has been informed of the student's rights under this title, if any, that will transfer to the student on reaching the age of majority under section 615(m).

(ii) RULE OF CONSTRUCTION—Nothing in this section shall be construed to require—

(I) that additional information be included in a student's IEP beyond what is explicitly required in this section; and

(II) the IEP Team to include information under 1 component of a student's IEP that is already contained under another component of such IEP.

(B) INDIVIDUALIZED EDUCATION PROGRAM TEAM—The term "individualized education program team" or "IEP Team" means a group of individuals composed of—

(i) the parents of a student with a disability;

(ii) not less than 1 general education teacher of such student (if the student is, or may be, participating in the general education environment);

(iii) not less than 1 special education teacher, or where appropriate, not less than 1 special education provider of such student;

(iv) a representative of the local educational agency who—

(I) is qualified to provide, or supervise the provision of, specially designed instruction to meet the unique needs of students with disabilities;

(II) is knowledgeable about the general education curriculum; and

(III) is knowledgeable about the availability of resources of the local educational agency;

(v) an individual who can interpret the instructional implications of evaluation results, who may be a member of the team described in clauses (ii) through (vi);

(vi) at the discretion of the parent or the agency, other individuals who have knowledge or special expertise regarding the student, including related services personnel as appropriate; and

(vii) whenever appropriate, the student with a disability.

(C) IEP TEAM ATTENDANCE—

(i) ATTENDANCE NOT NECESSARY—A member of the IEP Team shall not be required to attend an

IEP meeting, in whole or in part, if the parent of a student with a disability and the local educational agency agree that the attendance of such member is not necessary because the member's area of the curriculum or related services is not being modified or discussed in the meeting.

(ii) EXCUSAL—A member of the IEP Team may be excused from attending an IEP meeting, in whole or in part, when the meeting involves a modification to or discussion of the member's area of the curriculum or related services, if—

(I) the parent and the local educational agency consent to the excusal; and

(II) the member submits, in writing to the parent and the IEP Team, input into the development of the IEP prior to the meeting.

(iii) WRITTEN AGREEMENT AND CONSENT REQUIRED—A parent's agreement under clause (i) and consent under clause (ii) shall be in writing.

(D) IEP TEAM TRANSITION—In the case of a student who was previously served under part C, an invitation to the initial IEP meeting shall, at the request of the parent, be sent to the part C service coordinator or other representatives of the part C system to assist with the smooth transition of services.

(2) REQUIREMENT THAT PROGRAM BE IN EFFECT—

(A) IN GENERAL—At the beginning of each school year, each local educational agency, State educational agency, or other State agency, as the case may be, shall have in effect, for each student with a disability in the agency's jurisdiction, an individualized education program, as defined in paragraph (1)(A).

(B) PROGRAM FOR STUDENT AGED 3 THROUGH 5—In the case of a student with a disability aged 3 through 5 (or, at the discretion of the State educational agency, a 2-year-old student with a disability who will turn age 3 during the school year), the IEP Team shall consider the individualized family service plan that contains the material described in section 636, and that is developed in accordance with this section, and the individualized family service plan may serve as the IEP of the student if using that plan as the IEP is—

(i) consistent with State policy; and

(ii) agreed to by the agency and the student's parents.

(C) PROGRAM FOR STUDENTS WHO TRANSFER SCHOOL DISTRICTS—

(i) IN GENERAL—

(I) TRANSFER WITHIN THE SAME STATE—In the case of a student with a disability who transfers school districts within the same academic year, who enrolls in a new school, and who had an IEP that was in effect in the same State, the local educational agency shall provide such student with a free appropriate public education, including services comparable to those described in the previously held IEP, in consultation with the parents until such time as the local educational agency adopts the previously held IEP or develops, adopts, and implements a new IEP that is consistent with Federal and State law.

(II) TRANSFER OUTSIDE STATE—In the case of a student with a disability who transfers school districts within the same academic year, who enrolls in a new school, and who had an IEP that was in effect in another State, the local educational agency shall provide such student with a free appropriate public education, including services comparable to those described in the previously held IEP, in consultation with the parents until such time as the local educational agency conducts an evaluation pursuant to subsection (a)(1), if determined to be necessary by such agency, and develops a new IEP, if appropriate, that is consistent with Federal and State law.

(ii) TRANSMITTAL OF RECORDS—To facilitate the transition for a student described in clause (i)—

      (I) the new school in which the student enrolls shall take reasonable steps to promptly obtain the student's records, including the IEP and supporting documents and any other records relating to the provision of special education or related services to the student, from the previous school in which the student was enrolled, pursuant to section 99.31(a)(2) of title 34, Code of Federal Regulations; and

     (II) the previous school in which the student was enrolled shall take reasonable steps to promptly respond to such request from the new school.

(3) DEVELOPMENT OF IEP—

  (A) IN GENERAL—In developing each student's IEP, the IEP Team, subject to subparagraph (C), shall consider—

    (i)   the strengths of the student;
    (ii) the concerns of the parents for enhancing the education of their student;
    (iii) the results of the initial evaluation or most recent evaluation of the student; and
    (iv) the academic, developmental, and functional needs of the student.

  (B) CONSIDERATION OF SPECIAL FACTORS—The IEP Team shall—

    (i) in the case of a student whose behavior impedes the student's learning or that of others, consider the use of positive behavioral interventions and supports, and other strategies, to address that behavior;
    (ii) in the case of a student with limited English proficiency, consider the language needs of the student as such needs relate to the student's IEP;
    (iii) in the case of a student who is blind or visually impaired, provide for instruction in Braille and the use of Braille unless the IEP Team determines, after an evaluation of the student's reading and writing

skills, needs, and appropriate reading and writing media (including an evaluation of the student's future needs for instruction in Braille or the use of Braille), that instruction in Braille or the use of Braille is not appropriate for the student;

(iv) consider the communication needs of the student, and in the case of a student who is deaf or hard of hearing, consider the student's language and communication needs, opportunities for direct communications with peers and professional personnel in the student's language and communication mode, academic level, and full range of needs, including opportunities for direct instruction in the student's language and communication mode; and

(v) consider whether the student needs assistive technology devices and services.

(C) REQUIREMENT WITH RESPECT TO GENERAL EDUCATION TEACHER—A general education teacher of the student, as a member of the IEP Team, shall, to the extent appropriate, participate in the development of the IEP of the student, including the determination of appropriate positive behavioral interventions and supports, and other strategies, and the determination of supplementary aids and services, program modifications, and support for school personnel consistent with paragraph (1)(A)(i)(IV).

(D) AGREEMENT—In making changes to a student's IEP after the annual IEP meeting for a school year, the parent of a student with a disability and the local educational agency may agree not to convene an IEP meeting for the purposes of making such changes, and instead may develop a written document to amend or modify the student's current IEP.

(E) CONSOLIDATION OF IEP TEAM MEETINGS—To the extent possible, the local educational agency shall encourage the consolidation of reevaluation meetings for the student and other IEP Team meetings for the student.

(F) AMENDMENTS—Changes to the IEP may be made either by the entire IEP Team or, as provided in subparagraph (D), by amending the IEP rather than by redrafting the entire IEP. Upon request, a parent shall be provided with a revised copy of the IEP with the amendments incorporated.

(4) REVIEW AND REVISION OF IEP—

(A) IN GENERAL—The local educational agency shall ensure that, subject to subparagraph (B), the IEP Team—

(i) reviews the student's IEP periodically, but not less frequently than annually, to determine whether the annual goals for the student are being achieved; and

(ii) revises the IEP as appropriate to address—

(I) any lack of expected progress toward the annual goals and in the general education curriculum, where appropriate;

(II) the results of any reevaluation conducted under this section;

(III) information about the student provided to, or by, the parents, as described in subsection (c)(1)(B);

(IV) the student's anticipated needs; or

(V) other matters.

(B) REQUIREMENT WITH RESPECT TO GENERAL EDUCATION TEACHER—A general education teacher of the student, as a member of the IEP Team, shall, consistent with paragraph (1)(C), participate in the review and revision of the IEP of the student.

(5) MULTI-YEAR IEP DEMONSTRATION—

(A) PILOT PROGRAM—

(i) PURPOSE—The purpose of this paragraph is to provide an opportunity for States to allow parents and local educational agencies the opportunity for long-term planning by offering the option of developing a comprehensive multi-year IEP, not to exceed 3 years, that is designed to coincide with the natural transition points for the student.

(ii) AUTHORIZATION—In order to carry out the purpose of this paragraph, the Secretary is authorized to approve not more than 15 proposals from States to carry out the activity described in clause (i).

(iii) PROPOSAL—

(I) IN GENERAL—A State desiring to participate in the program under this paragraph shall submit a proposal to the Secretary at such time and in such manner as the Secretary may reasonably require.

(II) CONTENT—The proposal shall include—

(aa) assurances that the development of a multi-year IEP under this paragraph is optional for parents;

(bb) assurances that the parent is required to provide informed consent before a comprehensive multi-year IEP is developed;

(cc) a list of required elements for each multi-year IEP, including—

(AA) measurable goals pursuant to paragraph (1)(A)(i)(II), coinciding with natural transition points for the student, that will enable the student to be involved in and make progress in the general education curriculum and that will meet the student's other needs that result from the student's disability; and

(BB) measurable annual goals for determining progress toward meeting the goals described in subitem (AA); and

(dd) a description of the process for the review and revision of each multi-year IEP, including—

(AA) a review by the IEP Team of the student's multi-year IEP at each of the student's natural transition points;

(BB) in years other than a student's natural transition points, an annual review of the student's IEP to determine the student's current levels of progress and whether the annual goals for the student are being achieved, and a requirement to amend the IEP, as appropriate, to enable the student to continue to meet the measurable goals set out in the IEP;

(CC) if the IEP Team determines on the basis of a review that the student is not making sufficient progress toward the goals described in the multi-year IEP, a requirement that the local educational agency shall ensure that the IEP Team carries out a more thorough review of the IEP in accordance with paragraph (4) within 30 calendar days; and

(DD) at the request of the parent, a requirement that the IEP Team shall conduct a review of the student's multi-year IEP rather than or subsequent to an annual review.

(B) REPORT—Beginning 2 years after the date of enactment of the Individuals with Disabilities Education Improvement Act of 2004, the Secretary shall submit an annual report to the Committee on Education and the Workforce of the House of Representatives and the Committee on Health, Education, Labor, and Pensions of the Senate regarding the effectiveness of the program under this paragraph and any specific recommendations for broader implementation of such program, including—

    (i) reducing—

        (I) the paperwork burden on teachers, principals, administrators, and related service providers; and

        (II) noninstructional time spent by teachers in complying with this part;

    (ii) enhancing longer-term educational planning;

    (iii) improving positive outcomes for students with disabilities;

    (iv) promoting collaboration between IEP Team members; and

    (v) ensuring satisfaction of family members.

(C) DEFINITION—In this paragraph, the term "natural transition points" means those periods that are close in time to the transition of a student with a disability from preschool to elementary grades, from elementary grades to middle or junior high school grades, from middle or junior high school grades to secondary school grades, and from secondary school grades to post-secondary activities, but in no case a period longer than 3 years.

(6) FAILURE TO MEET TRANSITION OBJECTIVES—If a participating agency, other than the local educational agency, fails to provide the transition services described in the IEP in accordance with paragraph (1)(A)(i)(VIII), the local educational agency shall reconvene the IEP Team to identify alternative strategies to meet the transition objectives for the student set out in the IEP.

(7) STUDENTS WITH DISABILITIES IN ADULT PRISONS—

(A) IN GENERAL—The following requirements shall not apply to students with disabilities who are convicted as adults under State law and incarcerated in adult prisons:

    (i) The requirements contained in section 612(a)(16) and paragraph (1)(A)(i)(VI) (relating to participation of students with disabilities in general assessments).

    (ii) The requirements of items (aa) and (bb) of paragraph (1)(A)(i)(VIII) (relating to transition planning and transition services), do not apply with respect to such students whose eligibility under this part will end, because of such students' age, before such students will be released from prison.

(B) ADDITIONAL REQUIREMENT—If a student with a disability is convicted as an adult under State law and incarcerated in an adult prison, the student's IEP Team may modify the student's IEP or placement notwithstanding the requirements of sections 612(a)(5)(A) and paragraph (1)(A) if the State has demonstrated a bona fide security or compelling penological interest that cannot otherwise be accommodated.

(e) EDUCATIONAL PLACEMENTS—Each local educational agency or State educational agency shall ensure that the parents of each student with a disability are members of any group that makes decisions on the educational placement of their student.

(f) ALTERNATIVE MEANS OF MEETING PARTICIPATION— When conducting IEP team meetings and placement meetings pursuant to this section, section 615(e), and section 615(f)(1)(B), and carrying out administrative matters under section 615 (such as scheduling, exchange of witness lists, and status conferences), the parent of a student with a disability and a local educational agency may agree to use alternative means of meeting participation, such as video conferences and conference calls.

Glossary

Ability grouping. The grouping of students based on their achievement in an area of study.

Adaptive behavior. The collection of conceptual, social, and practical skills that people have learned so they can function in their everyday lives.

Age equivalent. A very general score that compares the performance of a student with others of the same age.

Age norms. Standards based on the average performance of individuals according to age groups.

Anecdotal record. A procedure for recording and analyzing observations of a student's behavior; an objective, narrative description.

Assessment. The collecting and analyzing of information about a student for the purpose of making decisions about the student's program of instruction.

At risk. Having a high potential for experiencing future medical or learning problems.

Attention deficit/hyperactivity disorder (ADHD). A psychiatric condition characterized by poor attention, distractibility, impulsivity, and hyperactivity.

Authentic assessment. A performance-based assessment technique on the basis of the student's application of knowledge to real-life activities, real-world settings, or a simulation of such settings using real-life, real-world activities.

Baseline measure. The level or frequency of behavior prior to the implementation of an instructional procedure that will later be evaluated.

Ceiling. The point in the administration of an educational assessment instrument at which the test-taker has made a predetermined number of errors, a preestablished criterion that suggests the test-taker has achieved a maximal expectable performance. At that point, no further items are administered.

Collection. The process of tracing and gathering information from many background sources on a student such as school records, observation, parent intakes, and teacher reports.

Construct validity. The extent to which a test measures the theoretical construct or attribute that it purports to measure.

Correlation. A co-occurrence in the behavior of two or more variables that suggests a meaningful relationship between the variables.

Criterion-referenced tests (CRTs). Tests that are scored according to a standard, or criterion, that the teacher, school, or test publisher decides represents an acceptable level of mastery.

Criterion-related validity. A demonstrated equivalence between an instrument and another known already to be a reliable measure of the same trait or skill.

Curriculum-based assessment (CBA). A direct evaluation of skills that form part of the test-taker's curriculum. "Tests" of performance in this case come directly from the curriculum.

Due process. The legal steps and processes outlined in educational law that protect the rights of students with disabilities.

Grade equivalent (GE). A measure of the score that would be achieved by students in the stated grade on the same instrument. For example, a GE of 6.2 identifies a score that would be achieved by students in the second month of grade 6 taking the same test. A very general score.

Hyperactivity. Behavior that is characterized by excessive motor activity or restlessness.

Impulsivity. Non-goal-oriented activity exhibited by individuals who lack careful thought and reflection prior to a behavior.

Individualized education program (IEP). A written educational program that outlines the current levels of performance, related services, educational goals, and modifications for a student with a disability. This plan is developed by a team including the student's parent(s), teacher(s), and support staff.

Informal tests. Assessment techniques that are not intended to provide a comparison to a broader group beyond the students in the local project.

Interrater reliability. A measure of the degree to which two raters independently would observe and record specified behaviors in the same way.

Intervention. Preventive, remedial, compensatory, or survival services made on behalf of an individual with a disability.

Least restrictive environment (LRE). An educational setting for exceptional students and students with disabilities that minimizes their exclusion from students without disabilities.

Mean. The mathematical average of the distribution of scores.

Median. The middle score in a distribution. It is the score that separates the top half of the test takers from the bottom half.

Mode. The score in the distribution that most frequently occurs.

Multidisciplinary teams (MDT). The collective efforts of individuals from a variety of disciplines in assessing the needs of a student. Also called an interdisciplinary team.

Native language. The primary language used by an individual.

Normal distribution. In a standardized test, an assumed pattern of scores that would occur if most test-takers achieved scores near the average, few test-takers achieved very high or very low scores, and all scores were distributed evenly above and below the mean.

Norm-referenced tests. Tests that compare a student's performance to the performance of others on the same measure.

Outcome-based assessment. The evaluation of skills that are important in real life.

Percentile rank (percentile). A score indicating the percentage of scores that occur at or below a given score. A percentile rank of 75 means a score as high as or higher than 75 percent of all test-takers.

Portfolio. A collection of (a student's) work samples, permanent products, and test results from a variety of instruments and measures.

Portfolio assessment. An assessment of a student's overall efforts, progress, and achievement in one or more areas based on work the student has produced during instruction.

Positive reinforcement. Any stimulus or event that occurs after a behavior has been exhibited that increases the possibility of that behavior occurring in the future.

Predictive validity. In testing, the degree to which performance on a test instrument can be counted on to resemble performance on some nontesting task. For example, the degree to which a student's performance on a mathematics test resembles a student's performance on actual mathematics tasks in the classroom.

Pupil personnel team. A group of professionals from the same school who meet at regular intervals to discuss students' problems and offer suggestions or directions for resolution.

Pupils with special educational needs (PSEN). Students defined as having mathematics and reading achievement lower than the 23rd percentile and requiring remediation. These students are not considered to have disabilities but are entitled to assistance to elevate their academic levels.

Raw score. The count of items correctly answered on a given test. In almost all cases, the raw score is the first score a teacher obtains when interpreting data.

Related services. Services provided to students with disabilities to enhance their ability to learn and function in the least restrictive environment. Such services may include in-school counseling and speech and language services.

Reliability. The degree to which a testing instrument would produce equivalent results over the course of repeated administrations.

Reliability coefficient. A statistical measure of the degree to which a testing instrument has produced equivalent results over the course of repeated administrations.

Reliable test scores. Test scores that produce similar scores across various conditions and situations, including different evaluators and testing environments.

Remediation. An educational program designed to teach students to overcome some deficit or disability through education and training.

Response to intervention (RTI). A three-tiered model established under IDEA 2004 as an alternative to the discrepancy model for determining whether a student has a learning disability.

Screening. The process of examining groups of students to identify at-risk students.

Split-half reliability. The comparison of a test-taker's performance on a randomly selected subset of half of a group of similar items is compared to the test-taker's performance on the other half of that group of items in order to assess the degree to which the test-taker's performance on similar items is in fact similar. The purpose is to assess whether the items expected to measure similar achievement or ability do in fact do so.

Standard deviation. A measure of the geometric distance of a given score from the mean. It is calculated by taking the square root of the variance.

Standard error of measurement (SEM). The expected range of variation in scores upon repeated administrations of a given instrument.

Standardized tests. Tests that compare the performance of each student with a representative group of students who take the same test, using detailed procedures for administration, timing, scoring, and interpretation procedures that must be followed precisely to obtain valid and reliable results.

Standard score. A score that has been transformed to fit a normal distribution curve.

Stanine. An abbreviation for *standard nines*; a standard score that has a mean of 5 and a standard deviation of 2. Stanine scores range from 1 to 9.

Task analysis. The breaking down of a particular task into its basic sequential steps, component parts, or the skills necessary to accomplish the task.

Test-retest reliability. The degree to which a similar test-taker can be expected to obtain the same score when tested during any other administration of the same test.

***T* scores.** A way to express test performance by means of standardized scores. *T* scores have a mean of 50 with a standard deviation of 10.

Validity. The extent to which a test measures what it is supposed to measure.

References and Suggested Readings

Assistance to States for the Education of Children With Disabilities, Preschool Grants for Children With Disabilities, and Early Intervention Program for Infants and Toddlers With Disabilities, Code of Federal Regulations 34, Proposed Rules, 62 Fed. Reg. 55,025–55,075 (October 22, 1997).

Baca, L. M., & Cervantes, H. T. (Eds.). (1989). *The bilingual special education interface* (2nd ed.). Columbus, OH: Merrill.

Bateman, B. D. (1997). *Better IEPs: How to develop legally correct and educational useful programs* (3rd ed.). Longmont, CO: Sopris West.

Berndt, S. (2000, December). *Statewide assessment and students with disabilities* (PowerPoint Presentation). Madison: Wisconsin Department of Public Instruction.

Braden, J., & Elliott, S. (2000). *Educational assessment and accountability for all students.* Madison: Wisconsin Department of Public Instruction.

Chambers, A. C. (1997). *Has technology been considered? A guide for IEP teams.* Albuquerque, NM: Council of Administrators of Special Education.

Chang, R. Y., & Kehoe, K. R. (1994). *Quality improvement series: Meetings that work.* Irvine, CA: Richard Chang Associates.

Collier, C., & Kalk, M. (1989). Bilingual special education curriculum development. In L. M. Baca & H. T. Cervantes (Eds.), *The bilingual special education interface* (2nd ed., pp. 205–229). Columbus, OH: Merrill.

Extended Year Special Education. Transparency. (1996). IEP training material. Mountain Plains Regional Resource Center, Drake University, IA.

Hoover, J. J., & Collier, C. (1989). Methods and materials for bilingual special education. In L. M. Baca & H. T. Cervantes (Eds.), *The bilingual special education interface* (2nd ed., pp. 231–255). Columbus, OH: Merrill.

Iowa Department of Education, Bureau of Special Education. (1998). *Their future . . . our guidance.* Des Moines, IA: Author.

Mason, C. Y., McGahee-Kovac, M., & Johnson, L. (2004, January–February). How to help students lead their IEP meetings. *Teaching Exceptional Students, 36*(3), 18–24.

Ortiz, A. A. (1997). *Second language acquisition.* Austin: University of Texas, College of Education.

Pub. L. No. 105-17, 111 Stat. 37 (1997). Individuals with Disabilities Education Act Amendments of 1997.

Saint, S., & Lawson, J. R. (1994). *Rules for reaching consensus: A modern approach to decision-making.* San Diego, CA: Pfeiffer.

Sopko, K. (2003). *The IEP: A synthesis of current literature since 1997.* Alexandria, VA: National Association of State Directors of Special Education.

Stainback, S., & Stainback, W. (1992). *Controversial issues confronting special education.* Boston: Allyn & Bacon.

Storms, J., O'Leary, E., & Williams, J. (2000, May). *Transition requirements: A guide for states, districts, schools, universities and families.* Minneapolis: University of Minnesota, Publications Office.

Takanishi, R. (2004). Leveling the playing field: Supporting immigrant students from birth to eight. *Future of Students, 14(2),* 61–79. Retrieved January 13, 2007, from http://www.futureofchildren.org/usr_doc/takanishi.pdf

Test, D. W., Mason, C., Hughes, C., et al. (2004). Student involvement in individualized education program meetings. *Exceptional Students 70*(4), 391–412.

U.S. Department of Education, Office of Special Education and Rehabilitative Services. (2000, July). *A guide to the individualized education program.* Retrieved August 23, 2005, from http://www.ed.gov/parents/needs/speced/iepguide/index.html

Vincent, L. J. (1994). *Ten strategies to enhance families as decision makers.* Helena, MT: Staff Development and Technical Assistance.

Wisconsin Department of Public Instruction. (1998). *Answers to frequently asked questions stemming from recent statutory changes* (DPI Update Bulletin No. 98.10). Madison, WI: Author.

Wisconsin Department of Public Instruction. (1998). *Guidelines for complying with the assessment provisions of the Individuals with Disabilities Education Act* (DPI Information Update Bulletin No. 98.14). Madison, WI: Author.

Wisconsin Department of Public Instruction. (1999). *Special education in plain language: A user-friendly handbook on special education laws, policies, and practices in Wisconsin.* Madison, WI: Author.

Wisconsin Department of Public Instruction. (2000, July). *Reference materials for the sample forms package.* Madison, WI: Author.

Wisconsin Department of Public Instruction. (2000, September). *Monitoring checklist.* Madison, WI: Author.

Wright, A., & Laffin, K. (2001). *A guide for writing IEPs.* Madison: Wisconsin Department of Public Instruction.

Zhang, C., & Bennett, T. (2003). Facilitating the meaningful participation of culturally and linguistically diverse families in the IFSP and IEP process. *Focus on Autism and Other Developmental Disabilities, 18*(1), 51–59.

Index

CORWIN PRESS

The Corwin Press logo—a raven striding across an open book—represents the union of courage and learning. Corwin Press is committed to improving education for all learners by publishing books and other professional development resources for those serving the field of PreK–12 education. By providing practical, hands-on materials, Corwin Press continues to carry out the promise of its motto: **"Helping Educators Do Their Work Better."**